ıg Pe⁓   ˙gend

DEVELOPING ASSESSMENT FOR
THE NATIONAL CURRICULUM

Bedford Way Series
Published by Kogan Page in association with the Institute of Education,
University of London

Developing Assessment for the National Curriculum Caroline Gipps
(ed.) *The National Curriculum and the Primary School* Jeni Riley (ed.)
English and the National Curriculum Ken Jones (ed.) *History in the
National Curriculum* Richard Aldridge (ed.) *Quality Assurance and
Accountability in Higher Education* Cari Loder (ed.) *Britain and a Single
Market Europe: Prospects for a common school curriculum* Martin
McLean *Financial Support for Students: grants, loans or graduate tax?*
Maureen Woodhall (ed.) *Looking, Making and Learning: Art in the
primary school* Anthony Dyson (ed.) *Personal and Social Education:
philosophical perspectives* Patricia White (ed.) *Reforming Religious
Education: the religious clauses of the 1988 Education Reform Act*
Edwin Cox and Josephine M Cairns *The National Curriculum* Denis
Lawton and Clyde Chitty (eds).

THE BEDFORD WAY SERIES

DEVELOPING ASSESSMENT FOR THE NATIONAL CURRICULUM

**Edited by
CAROLINE GIPPS**

Contributors:
**Margaret Brown, Tony Burgess, Shirley Clarke,
Caroline Gipps, Arthur Jennings, Denis Lawton,
Shelley McAlister, Bet McCallum, Kay Stables,
Gordon Stobart, Pat Tunstall**

KOGAN PAGE

Published in association with
The Institute of Education, University of London

First published in 1992

Apart from any fair dealing for the purposes of research or private study, or criticism or review, as permitted under the Copyright, Designs and Patents Act, 1988, this publication may only be reproduced, stored or transmitted, in any form or by any means, with the prior permission in writing of the publishers, or in the case of reprographic reproduction in accordance with the terms of licences issued by the Copyright Licensing Agency. Enquiries concerning reproduction outside those terms should be sent to the publishers at the undermentioned address:

Kogan Page Limited
120 Pentonville Road
London N1 9JN

© Institute of Education, 1992

British Library Cataloguing in Publication Data

A CIP record for this book is available from the British Library

ISBN 0 7494 0837 5

Typeset by Paul Stringer, Watford
Printed and bound in Great Britain by
Biddles Ltd, Guildford and Kings Lynn

Contents

Notes on Contributors

Margaret Brown is Professor of Mathematics Education at the Centre for Educational Studies, King's College London. She was a member of the Mathematics Curriculum Working Group and is one of the grant holders for the SEAC CATS KS3 Assessment Development, and is Co-director of the National Assessment in Primary Schools (NAPS) project.

Tony Burgess is Reader in Education and teaches in the Department of English, Media and Drama at the Institute of Education, University of London. He has written and researched in English teaching and was a part-time member of the English team, at Key Stage 3, in the Consortium for Assessment and Testing in Schools.

Shirley Clarke is the Co-ordinator for Assessment in the INSET Department of the Institute of Education. Before that, she was the Writing Team Co-ordinator of the CATS Key Stage 1 SAT Development Agency. She was originally a primary teacher and then an ILEA Primary Mathematics Consultant. She is about to publish *Formative Mathematics Assessment in the National Curriculum* and is co-author of *Headstart*, a home learning series for 5- to 9-year-olds.

Caroline Gipps is a Reader in Education at the Institute of Education, University of London. A primary teacher, psychologist and researcher by training, she has carried out a wide range of research on the uses and impact of assessment; she has published both in this area and in the critical evaluation of assessment developments. She will be President of BERA in 1992–3, and is Co-director of the NAPS project.

Arthur Jennings is a Senior Lecturer in Science Education at the Institute of Education, University of London. He worked part-time with the Key Stage 3 science SAT development team between 1989 and 1991.

Denis Lawton is Professor of Education in the Curriculum Studies Department of the Institute of Education, University of London. He is the author of several books on curriculum, including *Education, Culture and the National Curriculum* (Hodder, 1989).

Shelley McAlister, part-time research assistant, has experience in industrial and commercial research. She is a Tutor/Counsellor in Social Science at the Open University.

Bet McCallum, a former primary headteacher, is a course tutor to the Diploma in Education (Primary Schools) at the Institute of Education, University of London, and senior researcher to the NAPS project.

Kay Stables is Lecturer in the Department of Design Studies at Goldsmiths' College, University of London. Formerly a secondary school teacher, her recent principal professional interests have been in the area of design and technology and its assessment. From 1986 to 1990 she was Senior Researcher on the Assessment of Performance Unit's design and technology project, and from 1990 to 1992 she was Director of the CATS team developing, on behalf of SEAC, the non-statutory Standard Assessment Tasks for Key Stage 1 technology. She is joint author of *The Assessment of Performance in Design and Technology: the Final Report of the APU project* (HMSO).

Gordon Stobart is Head of Research at the University of London Examinations and Assessment Council (ULEAC). He is a former educational psychologist, with experience in both the UK and USA, and taught English for eight years.

Pat Tunstall has been Director of the London Record of Achievement Scheme since April 1990. Her team, based at the Institute of Education, has just produced *Primary Records of Achievement: A Teacher's Guide to Reviewing, Recording and Reporting* (Hodder and Stoughton, 1992). Before joining the Institute, she was a member of ILEA's Central Assessment Team.

Introduction

This collection of papers attempts to bring together researchers' accounts of the development of assessment for the National Curriculum. The development has been complicated and confused, and has caused many problems not only for test developers but also for teachers. As the following chapters make plain, considerable changes have been made to the original blueprint.

A brief history will help to set the context. In 1987 the Government announced its intention to have a system of national assessment to accompany the National Curriculum. In 1988 a blueprint for this assessment programme was published in the Report of the Task Group on Assessment and Testing (TGAT) (DES, 1988). In January 1989 development began on the Key Stage 1 assessments and in July 1989 the assessment programme for Key Stage 3 began. However, by the summer of 1992 the external assessment used at both of these Key Stages was quite different from that outlined in 1988 and developed in 1989. Most of the changes, and indeed the content of these papers, relate to the external Standard Assessment Tasks (SATs) which are to act as the reference point for continuous assessment by teachers. Over time the SATs are coming to deviate more and more from the original model outlined in the TGAT Report. Part of the role of this book is to explain how and why this has happened. This shift in the SAT model is important because, as with any significant external assessment, its style, mode and content will have a considerable impact on the teaching which leads up to it.

One might well ask why bother to analyse the 1991 SAT experience and the 1990 SAT development exercise when it is clear that the whole structure of SATs is changing. The answer is that this has been an extraordinary innovation and there is no doubt that there are lessons to be learnt from it. This is the only example of a nation-wide assessment of pupils on a criterion-referenced authentic or performance assessment model and there are clear implications for our understanding of the structure and working of this type of assessment. (Authentic or performance assessment is a term used in the USA to denote assessments which match learning goals and are therefore more valid than many standardized tests.) We must share this knowledge, not least with our colleagues in the USA who are trying to shift their assessment system away from a reliance on standardized tests (Resnick and Resnick, 1991; Shepard, 1991). We in the UK have always been more involved in open-ended assessment than the USA and have led the world in the development of various forms of educational assessment, such as the Assessment of Performance Unit, graded tests, course-work assessment in GCSE, profiles and records of achievement. The SAT was but the logical extension of this trend.

Gipps in another publication (Gipps, 1991) has put forward a range of reasons why the model on which the national assessment structure is based is in tension. Most significantly, the same assessment cannot be used for formative and evaluative purposes since these require different timing, different involvement of the teacher, and different use of results. The first chapter in this book gives us another reason why the tension has appeared in relation to the SAT in particular. Simply put, the main problem is that the SAT, as it was originally conceived, was never meant to test every pupil on every Attainment Target.

The TGAT model relied on teacher assessment as the main assessment device, with the SAT used to support and moderate this assessment. Many readers of the TGAT Report, myself included, understood it to mean that each SAT would be given to each pupil and the SAT result weighed up with the teacher assessment result to give a final figure. Over the years the use of the SATs would draw teacher assessment into line around a common standard. This indeed is how the Secretary of State has interpreted the role of SATs: that they be used to assess individual children and must therefore produce results which are reliable as well as valid at the individual level. Reliability is highly significant if assessment results are to be used to make comparisons of pupils and schools, in other words if assessment is to be used for summative and/or evaluative purposes. Margaret Brown points out that the authors of the TGAT Report never intended the SATs to be used to moderate results for individual children; they were to be used to moderate a teacher's overall results for a class. Here lies the real nub of the problem: if the SAT is only an overall moderating device, then it needs only to sample across Attainment Targets. If, however, it is to be used to confirm teacher assessment for each child then it has to cover every Attainment Target. The problem is that the SAT as originally conceived – i.e. packages of tasks administered through a range of modes, including practical, oral, extended and group tasks, to ensure validity and good curriculum backwash – is simply not appropriate for assessing literally hundreds of assessment points. As these chapters show, it becomes too time consuming for testing whole age groups of pupils, particularly at a certain point in time. For what is essentially survey testing, something quick and reliable is needed. The SAT model on the other hand is ideal for individual, formative and diagnostic assessment by teachers for their own purposes. Individual formative continuous assessment by teachers can then be summed up at the end of Key Stages to give summative information. In this country, however, we tend to take the view that summative assessment, particularly if it is also to be used for evaluative purposes or for certification and selection, must be taken out of the hands of teachers, as indeed it is with public examinations. Thus teacher assessment is not to be used at the end of the Key Stage because teacher assessment is liable to be unreliable and/or biased. So goes the argument. It is of course true that teachers do need some form of referencing if their standards are to be comparable across the country, which fairness and equity demand. At GCSE and A level, external markers and moderation processes have been developed to deal with this issue and it is widely accepted (though not necessarily on a particularly good basis) that this produces reliable judgements.

Given the problems of overload, there are three possible routes that could have been taken. First, the intention to assess every pupil at a certain point in time on the SATs could have been changed (as happened in Scotland), thereby allowing teachers to use the SATs, as and when they wish, to moderate their assessments. Second, the curriculum structure could have been simplified to reduce the number of assessment criteria. The third option was to move away from the SAT model towards one based more on 'paper and pencil' style assessment. A fourth option, of course, would be to trust teachers – with proper training and resource material – to make reliable professional assessments of pupils, which are summed up and reported at the end of each Key Stage with no external assessment. I do not include this as a serious option given the educational climate which we face at the moment, though it is used in other countries. Although many educationalists and teachers might prefer the first of these three options, and the second is clearly sensible (this is one of the perennial issues in developing criterion-referenced assessment, viz. the desired level of specificity or generality of the criteria on which the assessment is based), the third has been the politicians' preferred option, combined with elements of the second: reworking the maths and science curriculum in order to reduce the number of assessment criteria.

While educationalists may be worried, as are the authors of these papers, about the negative side effects of narrow forms of testing, the view of the Administration in 1990–92 and apparently many members of the public is, perhaps understandably, that we have brought the situation on ourselves through proposing and accepting a flawed model. No one of sound mind would think that it is appropriate for teachers of 6- and 7-year-old children to spend six weeks assessing these pupils when they may only have had five full terms of precious schooling. The notion that these SATs could be integrated into the normal teaching and learning process has been shown to be difficult and unlikely (see Chapter 6). The argument that more time should have been set aside for development is seen as special pleading. However, I would suggest that any test development specialist in the world would think it quite unlikely that any country could move forward on such a massive scale with a newly developed assessment system in such a short space of time. So, we have the worst of all worlds, with the model being pared back when in fact it would have been better to go back to the drawing board and start again, once the nub of the problem was exposed.

This book stands as a document of how the professionals involved in the early stages of SAT development interpreted their original brief and dealt with the changes that were imposed at a political and bureaucratic level. In addition, two chapters consider impact issues. One looks at the summer 1991 SATs' impact on Year 2 teachers, their assessment practice and school organization. The other looks at how the requirements and advice on recording and reporting have helped and hindered formative assessment by teachers. It outlines the extraordinarily difficult recording task for teachers within the complex assessment structure, which was undoubtedly made worse by the lack of good advice. In the five chapters which relate to SAT development, several issues keep surfacing. Among these are: those to do with reliability and validity (crucial in any assessment development); the difficulties of interpretation of Statements of Attainment (the assessment criteria in what is supposed to be a criterion-referenced assessment system); manageability issues for teachers; and the effects on teaching and learning of a particular style of SAT. As the chapter dealing with the development of non-statutory SATs at Key Stage 1 makes clear, when the SATs are non-statutory many of these difficulties are diminished although they clearly do not disappear. The non-statutory SATs can clearly have a more supportive curriculum role and help develop teachers' skills in those areas. The fear is always that narrow 'paper and pencil' type tests will not extend teachers' skills and competencies but narrow them. This has happened in the past and there is no reason to suspect that it will not happen again. The final chapter presents a view of what remains of worth three years on from the TGAT Report. Although the author tries to be positive and optimistic, he is not entirely successful.

The purpose of this book is to give an account of how good intentions were diverted, and also to put down on record for test developers in other countries the complexities of developing criterion-referenced assessment on an authentic or performance model across a wide age range for all abilities. It was never likely to be easy, even without political interference, and these papers show that indeed it was not.

However, problems relating to the complexity of the underlying curriculum structure, the inappropriateness of this model for what was in effect a national survey, and a harsh political climate, should not divert us from our search for good quality educational assessment. Nor should the problems of development divert us from our message that good-quality educational assessment is the best way forward.

References

DES (1988) *The National Curriculum Task Group on Assessment and Testing: A Report*. DES/WO.

Gipps, C. (1991) 'Editorial.' *Cambridge Journal of Education*, Vol. 21, No. 2.

Resnick, L. and Resnick, D. (1991) 'Assessing the Thinking Curriculum: new tools for educational reform.' In: Gifford, B. and O'Connor, M. (eds), *Future Assessments*. Kluwer Academic Publishers.

Shepard, L. (1991) 'Interview on Assessment Issues with Lorrie Shepard.' *Educational Researcher*, Vol. 20, No. 2, March 1991.

Chapter One
Elaborate Nonsense?
The Muddled Tale of Standard
Assessment Tasks in Mathematics at
Key Stage 3

Margaret Brown

Introduction: Influences on policy

The real problem about the design of Standard Assessment Tasks (SATs), which contribute to the summative phases of National Curriculum assessment, is that there has not been a consistent official policy with regard to either what they should be like or what they are for.

The educational establishment, apart from a few dissenters (e.g. Howson, 1989; Goldstein, 1991), was initially willing to support the line taken in the Report of the Task Group on Assessment and Testing (TGAT) (DES, 1988a), not as ideal, but as representing the best proposal that was likely to be politically acceptable at the time. Due to a variety of reasons, including political shifts, misunderstanding, distrust and sheer haste, the TGAT recommendations were not fully implemented. Policy changes led to unnecessarily complex pilots, especially at Key Stage 1, which have resulted in increasing fragmentation of views on national assessment among the educational profession.

In contrast, the Centre for Policy Studies has been entirely consistent throughout in demanding uniform written tests of basic skills in the 3Rs at age 7, 11 and 14. Ministers, on seeing the bureaucratic products resulting from the policies adopted by their predecessors, have become increasingly inclined to espouse these simplistic views.

The account below traces these policy shifts and examines their effect on one particular aspect of national assessment, the design of SATs in mathematics at Key Stage 3 (KS3).

Background: The TGAT view of the nature and function of SATs
The Report, and more particularly the first of the three Supplementary Reports of TGAT (DES, 1988b), trod a careful, and hence not always clearly delineated, path along the boundaries of what would be acceptable to both the then Secretary of State for Education, Kenneth Baker, and the profession.

The view of the Group can be discerned to be that the major instrument of assessment was to be teacher assessment (TA) and that the chief purpose of SATs was to ensure comparability in the standards of TA, acting at the level of the class results rather than those of the individual child. For example, the Reports demonstrate how, for each of a small number of reporting elements ('profile components') in each subject, the class distribution of levels arrived at by TA was to be compared with the class distribution of SAT levels. Where there was a significant difference in distributions, the TA levels were to be adjusted. The only exception to this was where the lack of correspondence was found more generally, in which case the validity of the SAT used would be questioned. All these procedures were to take place at moderation meetings, in which teachers from a variety of schools would have been able to discuss their standards and agree their results with a moderator.

It is at the level of the results of the individual pupil that TGAT was necessarily rather more equivocal. In the Report it is suggested that in the (hopefully) small number of cases where the TA and SAT levels were found to differ for a profile component, more evidence would have to be sought to resolve the position. This was the only way out of a dilemma; to take either the SAT or TA level as overriding the other would have rendered the solution unacceptable both to politicians and teachers. In the first of the Supplementary Reports this procedure is elaborated on in that it is proposed that the quality of the evidence gathered to arrive at the TA level is taken into account retrospectively by the moderation meetings. None of the TGAT Reports suggests a procedure for adjusting individual levels where a discrepancy is found in the class distributions; this is left to the moderation meetings.

Thus in the TGAT proposals SATs were not required to give a completely reliable result for each profile component for each individual, but only a reasonably reliable overall distribution for the class.

Furthermore, in view of the large number of Attainment Targets (ATs) that TGAT knew were then being discussed by the Mathematics and Science Working Groups, TGAT proposed that at KS3 SATs be only required to sample across the ATs in each of between four and six coherent profile components defined for reporting purposes in each subject. (At the primary level it is worth remembering that TGAT proposed that profile components common to different subjects should be defined to ensure that there would be a much smaller overall number; the diagram in para. 121 suggests a total of about four reporting elements at the end of KS1, and 14 at the end of KS2. In reality, in the first national KS1 assessment in 1991, teachers were required to report on 32 separate elements in the core subjects alone.)

Also, the nature of SATs was discussed by TGAT and, in the appendix, examples of possible tasks were given. It was felt that, to ensure maximum validity, the SATs should take a variety of forms, including practical, oral, extended and group tasks.

This detail about the proposals made by TGAT has been included to demonstrate that many of the problems over national assessment have arisen not because of TGAT itself, but because official policy has departed from the original recommendations.

The KS3 SAT specifications: first departures from the TGAT model

By April 1989, when the specifications for the KS3 contracts were released from the School Examinations and Assessment Council (SEAC) for the first five subjects (mathematics, science, English, design & technology and Welsh), it was clear that there were already a number of significant departures from the TGAT model.

The first change, even more cogently expressed in SEAC advice to the Secretary of State dated 13 July 1989, was that assessment, moderation and reporting were to operate for all pupils at individual AT level. This decision was presumably made to meet the requirements of the 1988 Act to report 'in relation to the ATs', although at the time of TGAT it was considered by the DES that reporting with respect to profile components, defined by clusters of ATs, would satisfy this need. The change to AT reporting meant that new and complex forms of aggregation would be necessary in order also to generate results for individual pupils at both profile component and subject level. (TGAT had recommended individual reporting at profile component level only, with subject aggregation only for whole classes, using a mean rounded to one decimal place.)

Reporting at AT level made a nonsense of the proposals of the Mathematics Working Group, which had recommended assessment by SAT, and final reporting, only under three profile components, two content and one process. The 15 ATs (later reduced to 14 under two more-or-less meaningless profile components as the result of unhelpful interference from the DES/NCC) had been intended only as useful descriptions of coherent strands of development within the three profile components, and not as reporting elements which each required reliable assessment. (A similar situation pertained in science.)

Further, the development agencies at KS3 (as at KS1) were exhorted to provide SAT results for all 14 ATs; only 'should development agencies consider that time or other constraints make it impracticable for each pupil to be tested by SAT on all ATs in each subject' (para. 7 of the KS3 specification), were they allowed to propose an alternative arrangement.

The July 1989 SEAC advice incorporated the demise of moderation meetings and the 'preferral' of SAT to TA results where both existed. This led to a requirement of reliability for individual pupils' SAT results for each AT that no agency could reasonably satisfy.

The result was that the roles of TA and SAT had become reversed from that in the TGAT model; SATs were now seen not as providing a moderation instrument for checking the broad comparability of TA, but as providing reliable results for individual pupils on most ATs. The role of TA was reduced mainly to a device for entering pupils for the correct range of levels of SAT assessment.

The development agencies commissioned for mathematics and science at KS3 were thus faced with an extraordinarily difficult brief. The specification required them to provide, within less than a year, SAT packages for large-scale trials which would:

- assess validly and reliably at each of the levels 1 to 10 in each of many ATs tested;
- permit pupils to demonstrate achievement up to the highest level of which they are capable (this was taken for practical purposes to require a range of three levels, centring on the TA level agreed, for each AT);
- allow for pupils achieving different attainment levels in different ATs;
- cover as wide a range of ATs in each profile component as possible for individual pupils, and cover all ATs taken over the full SAT collection;
- include oral, practical and graphic work, done individually or in groups, and individual written tests in all ATs for which it was not obviously inappropriate;
- enable all pupils with special educational needs, except those for whom specific disapplication had been agreed, to participate;
- be free of ethnic and gender bias, and be available in Welsh;
- motivate pupils and engage their interest; and

- be easily administered, assessed and recorded by teachers (in practice taking less than 12 hours of class time), using resources that were normally available in secondary schools.

The first pilot phase (July 1989 – August 1990): Developing a viable model

The sole contract for KS3 SATs in mathematics was awarded to the London University Consortium for Assessment and Testing in Schools (CATS) and was to start in July 1989. CATS was also successful in obtaining not just the sole science contract, but also contracts in English and design & technology (later, technology). The mathematics team was led by Gill Close and, like the science team, was based at the Centre for Educational Studies at King's College London. The remaining teams were based with the other consortium partners, English at the Institute of Education, and technology at Goldsmiths' College, with a central team working from the publisher Hodder and Stoughton. The fifth partner, the University of London Examinations and Assessment Council (ULEAC), gave access to examination board expertise and data.

Although the mathematics SATs were developed by a team of around five experienced mathematics teachers working from King's College, some of the ideas were generated and given early classroom trials by a much larger team of teachers who met weekly.

The CATS maths team came to some quick decisions in order to satisfy what appeared to be the almost impossible brief.

1. Content/process integration

The Non-Statutory Guidance in Mathematics states that 'work related to Attainment Targets 2–8 and 10–14 cannot be satisfactorily pursued independently from that related to Attainment Targets 1 and 9' (the process targets) and, conversely, 'Attainment Targets 1 and 9 cannot be tackled in isolation from the rest...' (NCC, 1989, p. D2).

The decision was therefore made by the SATs team to assess the content ATs which were selected from ATs 2–8 and 10–14 in the context of ATs 1 and 9, i.e. while 'using and applying mathematics ... in practical tasks, in real-life problems, and to investigate within mathematics itself' (DES, 1989). This format would also allow the requirements for practical work to be met.

In such open tasks, pupils would not only have to demonstrate competence in relation to a Statement of Attainment, but would need in addition to be able to identify that this knowledge or skill was appropriate and to apply it in a particular open context. This was seen as an advantage in that it provided greater reliability and validity in the assessment of content statements.

Unlike the KS1 teams, the KS3 maths team already had considerable experience of assessing mathematics content during open tasks since most of its members had been involved in the development and piloting of such activities by the Graded Assessment in Mathematics (GAIM) project (1988).

The four SATs selected for the first trials in June 1990 were:

- *Packaging Marbles* – investigating possible designs for a pack to hold 10 marbles;
- *Grid Patterns* – exploring multiplication patterns on different number grids with the optional assistance of a computer;
- *Food Stall* – organizing and costing the running of a stall at a charity fair, including surveying customer preferences; and
- *Push Penny* – investigating the effects of using different board layouts for this game.

2. *Differentiation mainly by outcome*

This decision, namely to embed the assessment in relatively open tasks in which pupils have some choice over which direction they will follow, allowed differentiation by outcome among the ten levels to be adopted as the main, but not sole, method of differentiation.

It would have been difficult in any case to opt for differentiation by task. Although the SAT specification had proposed a collection of tests, each centring on one of the levels between 2 and 9, this assumed that pupils were expected to attain the same level in each AT. Early survey results suggested a wide spread for many pupils; recent 1991 results for over 11,000 Year 9 pupils confirm that for only 25 per cent of pupils did the results of TA for all the 14 ATs lie within a three-level spread (e.g. levels 3, 4 and 5), and indeed for 43 per cent they crossed a band of five or more levels. In these circumstances the logistics for teachers of getting the right level of task for each child on each separate AT would have proved almost impossible. (Experience during the KS1 pilot confirmed the difficulty when only three of the ten levels are in play.)

Moreover, a task which was broadly similar for all pupils would render the classroom management much simpler for teachers in mixed ability classes, and would have the advantage of encouraging pupils with special educational needs who could be working on the same task as all other pupils. It would also enable some group work to take place which could be used to satisfy the oral requirement in the specification.

Both of the above decisions were also arrived at by most of the CATS KS3 subject teams; indeed they had also been used by the CATS KS1 team for which the contract was prematurely terminated in 1990. One of the factors in the preferral of a rival KS1 group may have been official unease with this model.

3. Demonstrating achievement

The major problem of using an open task for an assessment in which a pupil gets only one chance is that pupils, in selecting a strategy for solving a problem or carrying out an investigation, may fail to demonstrate their highest level of ability. This was highlighted earlier by Denvir, Brown and Eve (1987) in their feasibility study for national assessment in mathematics at age 11.

Two ways of combating this problem were tried in the maths SATs. The first, more traditional, method introduced a more structured element into some of the tasks which required rather different activities to be undertaken by pupils in different bands of achievement. Sometimes this was presented as a conscious choice – for example, students were guided towards different types of snacks in the Food Stall work according to the difficulty of handling the quantities required, ranging from counting sausages and rolls for hot dogs at level 1 to calculating metric/imperial equivalents and complex recipe ratios for halva at level 6 and above. In other examples, the challenges got progressively harder, the higher ability students being expected to progress quickly through the earlier stages and tackle the more difficult sections that other students would not reach. (This strategy, beloved of examiners, was generally less successful than one requiring a guided choice.)

The second method of encouraging students to demonstrate their highest level of attainment was more radical, and reflected experience of successful negotiated student self-assessment gained within some Graded Assessment in Mathematics (GAIM) schools and/or those using well-designed Records of Achievement in mathematics. Each student was presented with a Personal Target Check (PTC) listing National Curriculum Statements of Attainment in an appropriate range of levels in the ATs being assessed by the task. The Statements of Attainment (SoAs) were translated into readily understandable language; where possible they were related to the task. For example in AT2 (Number) pupils were able to note and check off in their own PTC list some of the attainments they must demonstrate in order to gain the appropriate levels, such as: 'I have counted objects or pictures of food' (Level 1): and 'I have compared amounts written in decimals, like unit prices' (Level 6). Pupils used to negotiated assessment in Records of Achievement schemes were, not surprisingly, able to use such statements more effectively than those who had not previously been involved in trying to describe their own mathematical attainment.

4. Sampling of ATs
Different models of sampling of ATs were tried in the various Mathematics SATs in 1990.

At one extreme was the new model favoured by SEAC/DES in which all, or almost all, SoAs within each level of the selected ATs were assessed. This was the case in Push Penny which focused on AT14 (Probability) and AT9 (Process). The CATS teams in both science and mathematics concluded that in contradiction to SEAC/DES advice, it was impossible to assess reliably more than a few ATs in this concentrated way in a single SAT. This model also led to very contrived questions to cover those SoAs which did not form a consistent progression with the remainder, since such SoAs did not readily connect with any task which was constructed to assess the main strands of development within the AT.

Other pilot SATs were closer to the TGAT model in that they sampled across a larger number of ATs but did not provide comprehensive coverage of SoAs in each AT (except for the process ATs). In some cases the SATs focused on different ATs at different levels: for example Food Stall sampled from ATs 2, 3 and 4 (Number), AT 8 (Measures) and AT 12 and 13 (Data Handling) as well as ATs 1 and 9 (Process). This less strict requirement on coverage led to broader and more coherent tasks.

The results of the 1990 Pilot were broadly similar to those for 1991; in general they demonstrated the feasibility of this type of SAT, but highlighted some aspects in which improvements should be made.

The second pilot phase (September 1990–August 1991): Refining and modifying the model
One less than helpful policy requirement was re-affirmed for the 1991 pilot, namely that there should be comprehensive coverage of the SoAs in a small number of ATs, thus introducing more artificiality into the tasks themselves.

A further requirement was also imposed for all subjects at the request of the then Secretary of State, Kenneth Clarke. This was that there should be an element of written testing, taken under controlled conditions, for all pupils in each AT tested (except in oral and process ATs where it was obviously inappropriate).

The CATS mathematics team realized that the integrity of the tasks could be better retained by satisfying both of these requirements simultaneously. Thus written tests were formed which mainly focused on SoAs which were not likely to be demonstrated in an unforced way within the main task. Every effort was made however to ensure that the written tests were related to the main theme of the SAT.

Two mathematics SATs were developed and piloted in 1991. One, Gift Packs, was a refinement of the Packaging Marbles task the previous year, but this time the shape to be packaged was to be constructed from 12 connecting prisms. A new task, Octagon Loops, required an investigation of the various shapes which could be made from sets of octagonal tiles arranged in a contiguous pattern with a single central 'hole' (see Figure 1.1).

Both tasks were essentially similar to those used in 1990, but with a greater degree of structure. For example, Octagon Loops had four parts:

> In part 1, pupils work in groups to familiarize themselves with the rules for forming octagon loops by making some loops. The recording of these loops is shared by the group.

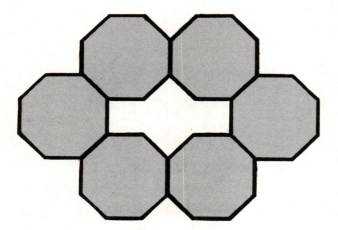

Figure 1.1 One possible Octagon Loop

In part 2, pupils carry out a number investigation based on the number of tiles used and the number of free edges in each loop.

In part 3, pupils consider some of the shape aspects of their octagon loops, with lower attainers identifying shapes and angles while higher attainers work on a shape investigation.

In part 4, pupils work on some short written questions appropriate to the levels they are attaining. These are presented in question and answer booklets, containing questions for individual SoAs which are grouped into bands of levels...

(Teachers' Notes for Octagon Loops)

An optional information technology (IT) element was also included.

The Octagon Loop task assessed ATs 1 and 9 (Process), AT 5 (Number Patterns) and AT 10 (Shape), at all levels from 1 to 10 in each case.

The different versions of part 4 ranged from that for levels 2–4, with one question on shape sorting, to that for levels 7–10 with 11 questions involving, for example, converging sequences of nested octagons (see Figure 1.2), or the application of the sine/cosine rules and circle theorems to calculate unknown sides and angles in the patterns on the octagons.

These two tasks were trialled in Summer 1991 in 161 schools in 34 LEAs, with approximately 20,000 pupils in 920 teaching groups. Ten per cent of the pupils were from ethnic minorities. The sample included 13 special schools representing a variety of types; altogether 9 per cent of the sample was reported as having special educational needs, and 2 per cent of these had statements.

Figure 1.2 A converging sequence of nested octagons

Many aspects of the detailed findings of the 1991 pilot reported by the team (CATS, 1991) are of interest but it will only be possible to provide a brief summary here.

The distribution of levels in the SAT results was very close to those predicted by TGAT (the mean SAT subject levels were 5.1 and 5.4 for Gift Packs and Octagon Loops respectively, against an expected mean of 5.5). The correlation between SAT levels and TA levels for separate ATs varied between 0.54 and 0.70, which seemed acceptable. As in KS1, the mean TA levels were higher than the SAT levels for all the mathematical content targets assessed, and particularly so in number calculations; the SAT levels were however higher for the process ATs. There was thus little difference between TA and SAT results for pupils' overall subject levels in mathematics.

Although many pupils were unfamiliar with aspects of the SAT (over 75 per cent had done little or no group, practical or open-ended work in maths), 87 per cent said that they had enjoyed some or all of the work. This is confirmed by the fact that 98 per cent of mainstream teachers (87 per cent of those in special schools) agreed that their pupils had engaged with the activity undertaken. Moreover 77 per cent of teachers, 86 per cent of observers and 90 per cent of pupils felt that they had learnt some mathematics during the SAT, an important fact since the SATs occupied up to three weeks of teaching time. In fact teachers reported that even lower sets sustained their interest over this period; for each task more than three times as many pupils wanted the activity to extend for a longer period as thought the SAT was too long.

More than 87 per cent of pupils were reported by observers to be using their PTC booklets effectively, although less than a quarter of classes had had previous experience of self-assessment. However, even with improvements from 1990, the language in the booklets was causing problems at lower levels.

Manageability of SATs had proved to be an issue at KS1. However, at KS3 teachers reported that the SAT took no more preparation time than normal work and, although it took rather more time to assess than normal (27 minutes per pupil against 21), this was still less than that for GCSE coursework (29 minutes). And this was in spite of the fact that 42 per cent of teachers reported that they had no experience of assessing against any form of criteria. The major source of difficulty in assessment was said to be the need to assess some parts of the SAT during class time, which only 49 per cent of teachers found manageable, although it was agreed to be more accurate and beneficial than written assessment.

New policies and new contracts: Changes for 1992 SATs
Between the time when pilot teachers received their INSET in late spring 1991 and when they administered the SATs in the summer, the pilot KS3 SATs for mathematics and science were shown by SEAC officials to the then Secretary of State, Kenneth Clarke. On leaving the meeting, he expressed the opinion that the SATs were 'elaborate nonsense', a remark which was widely reported in the press.

In July 1991, just one month before the full reports of the trials were due to be completed, the Secretary of State announced the termination of all the KS3 SATs contracts more than a year before they were due to end. Although it was first thought that the contracts would be renegotiated to a new specification with the existing agencies, it was confirmed on 31 July that they would be put out to open tender at the request of the Secretary of State.

In the event the CATS mathematics team retained the contract, but other subject teams within the Consortium lost their contracts, in most cases to examination boards who put in much lower bids.

The new specification requires three one-hour tests, covering between them all the content ATs. Process will be assessed by non-statutory SATs.

At the beginning of 1991 it had been announced that the Secretary of State required for assessment purposes a revision of all the ATs in mathematics and science to be in law by late 1991. This was mainly to enable the reduction in the number of reporting units which TGAT had previously achieved – and the DES rejected – by the use of profile components only. The revision was to be in time for the 1992 SATs to be set on the new Orders, although these would not be available until early 1992. The 1992 pilot could not therefore be statutory as planned since the new Orders could not formally come into force in schools before September 1992.

Items are being set for more than half the SoAs at each level, and pupils will only sit papers covering an appropriate range of four levels. These constraints allow approximately six minutes for pupils to demonstrate evidence on each SoA, and less than half a minute for a teacher to evaluate the evidence.

Teachers will not see the papers beforehand, although LEA and examination board personnel will.

The irony of this decision to revert to short written tests is that they are purported to be in the interest of teachers who, it was assumed – before waiting for the evidence to the contrary to become available – would find the KS3 SATs unmanageable and disruptive.

In fact teachers felt that the least satisfactory part of the 1991 pilot SATs were the written tests; these were thought to be contrived compared with the rest of the SAT and the majority of teachers, observers and experts felt they had not been a good way of assessing students' attainment levels. This was in contrast with the remainder of the SATs; the proportion of experts who agreed that the overall tasks set in 1991 provided valid assessment of the National Curriculum reached a hundred per cent for Octagon Loops and 91 per cent for Gift Packs. The reliability in terms of marker/remarker correspondence was also lowest in the written test part.

This means that, for no good reason, the decision has been made to go ahead with a form of testing which has already been demonstrated to be less popular with teachers and pupils, less valid and less reliable than that used in the 1991 pilot. Not only that, but there are also fears about the effect on bilingual pupils and those with special educational needs, who may not be properly catered for in written tests.

However, the most important effects are likely to be in the narrowing of the mathematics curriculum and the type of fragmented teaching and outright coaching to which written testing is likely to lead. The 1982 Cockcroft Report outlined the lack of confidence in, and understanding of, mathematics which had resulted from the adoption of this form of assessment in the past. The same political party which welcomed that report has now rejected its recommendations in favour of those simplistic views put to it by the members of extreme right wing groups such as the Centre for Policy Studies.

Thus the muddle of official misunderstanding and ill-judged policy reversals which has accompanied the development of assessment at KS3 now looks likely to reproduce the low standards and poor attitudes to mathematics that the National Curriculum was originally intended to reverse. This is made all the more frustrating for those involved not just because of the manifest waste of everyone's time, but also because they have caught a glimpse of something better which, as with so many other leading British developments, will be left for other countries to build on.

References

CATS (1991) *Mathematics KS3 Team: Report of 1991 Pilot*. London University Consortium for Assessment and Testing in Schools.

Denvir, B., Brown, M. and Eve, P. (1987) *Attainment Targets and Assessment in the Primary Phase: Mathematics Feasibility Study*. Department of Education and Science.

Department of Education and Science (1988a) *Task Group on Assessment and Testing: A Report.* DES/WO.

Department of Education and Science (1988b) *Task Group on Assessment and Testing: Three Supplementary Reports.* DES/WO.

Department of Education and Science and the Welsh Office (1989) *Mathematics in the National Curriculum.* DES/WO, HMSO.

GAIM Team (1988) *Graded Assessment in Mathematics Development Pack.* Macmillan Education.

Goldstein, H. (1991) *Assessment in Schools: an Alternative Framework.* Institute of Public Policy Research Paper.

Howson, G. (1989) *Maths Problem: Can More Pupils Reach Higher Standards?* Centre for Policy Studies Paper 102.

National Curriculum Council (1989) *Mathematics Non-Statutory Guidance.* NCC.

Chapter Two
Seeing the Wood for the Trees: The Assessment of Science at Key Stage 3

Arthur Jennings

Curriculum goals

According to the TGAT Report, assessment 'should be the servant, not the master, of the curriculum' (DES, 1988a). To achieve this laudable end, the goals of the curriculum must be fully understood so that appropriate assessment tools can be developed. In practice national curriculum science has suffered from varying degrees of uncertainty, especially amongst teachers, about the curriculum structure, its aims and assessment. The reasons for these uncertainties are not hard to find. They are attributable to the scope, nature and speed of the changes teachers have been required to implement.

The report of the National Curriculum Science Working Group was published for consultation in August 1988 (DES, 1988b). The synthesis of so much diverse science into one broad, balanced curriculum, structured to provide continuity and progression, was a singular achievement. Suddenly teachers, many of whom were still engaged in teaching separate science courses, found that the much discussed, far-reaching and long-term aspirations expressed in *Science 5–16: A Statement of Policy* (DES, 1985) had been translated into proposals for imminent implementation. Furthermore, secondary teachers familiar with syllabus statements issued by GCSE boards but with only a superficial knowledge of TGAT's plan found difficulty in interpreting the science curriculum proposals presented in 22 Attainment Targets (ATs), each with many Statements of Attainment (SoAs) all arranged in a hierachy of ten levels. The programmes of study which had a more accessible format were obscured amongst pages of SoAs which were to operate as assessment criteria. To secondary teachers long conditioned to believe that what is assessed is important, the SoAs stood out as dominant, individual 'trees' which obscured the curriculum 'wood' prescribed by the programmes of study.

Curriculum structure
The statutory science curriculum (DES, 1989) laid before Parliament in March 1989 contained a reduced number of ATs. Nevertheless the 17 ATs remaining included almost 400 SoAs. The two very unequal profile components (PCs) largely separated science process from science knowledge. Profile component 1 had only one AT (AT1); the rest were all in profile component 2. However, AT17 (The Nature of Science) appeared to fit more closely with AT1 since both of them offered approaches to teaching the content of ATs 2 to 16. Some ATs were constructed from content already well established within science curricula but aspects of earth science, human influence on the earth, astronomy and information technology represented new territory for many teachers.

A priority task in science departments was to restructure science courses to incorporate the new material from the programmes of study and to acquire additional apparatus and texts to support teaching. Since a time-lag was provided before the statutory requirement to carry out teacher assessment (TA) and since SATs were to be developed and trialled for two years before a first unrecorded run, assessment took a back seat for many teachers. Despite this apparent relegation of action on assessment, SoAs often dominated teachers' perspectives at the expense of programmes of study.

Early development work towards SATs
Those whose minds were focused on assessment, namely newly appointed LEA assessment co-ordinators, some science advisers and especially the KS3 SAT writing team, first engaged in looking at 'the wood' and its component 'trees'. This analytical appraisal of the detailed structure of the curriculum began to reveal some of the technical problems that would need to be addressed in the assessment programme. We shall consider some of these factors because they substantially influenced the way SAT assessment developed during 1990 and 1991. This will in turn affect future SAT and teacher assessment.

Each AT was sorted into conceptual strands. Some of them included several distinct strands of content but these were rarely continuous across several levels (see Essex LEA, 1991). AT3 (Processes of Life) illustrates this complexity with strands on animal and plant structure, life processes, the human life-cycle and health education. Indicators of progression were evident in some of these strands across a few contiguous levels but not through all the levels. The Education Reform Act requires that each pupil's performance be reported by AT level. Therefore an assessment approach that uses open-ended tasks to enable pupils to demonstrate their individual levels of achievement is an attractive option. This is called differentiation by outcome. When it was shown that content strands did not appear continuously through the levels this mode of differentiation was seen to offer very limited possibilities because, for example, a pupil who just failed to achieve at level 5 might drop down to level 3 simply because there was no criterion statement at level 4.

Analysis of ATs also showed that many of the SoAs contained several attributes. Again an example from AT3 illustrates this characteristic.

> *1989 Science AT3, 4b*: Know about the factors which contribute to good health and body maintenance, including the defence systems of the body, balanced diet, oral hygiene and avoidance of harmful substances such as tobacco, alcohol and other drugs.

To the assessor this SoA poses a series of problems. How many of these attributes must a pupil 'know about' to demonstrate achievement at this level? How exactly are the words 'know about the factors' to be interpreted. The Science Working Group had defined its use of the terms 'know about' and 'understand' but the Order showed no such consistency. Moreover a substantial measure of professional judgement was necessary to interpret many of the SoAs in the context of the level at which they appeared.

AT3,4b demonstrates another issue. 'Know about the defence systems of the body' at level 4 can only be clarified by reference to the programmes of study for KS2 and KS3 which spell out what pupils should be taught. Realistic interpretation depends on discovering what a wide range of pupils can achieve when they have been taught this curriculum content.

Appropriate interpretation of criteria was even necessary for some of the apparently precise SoAs. For example:

> *1989 Science AT1, 3e*: Quantify variables to the nearest labelled division of simple measuring instruments, for example, a rule.

Small-scale research carried out with Year 9 pupils showed that if the criterion of measuring to one millimetre divisions was applied then few KS3 pupils would achieve it. Measurement to the nearest centimetre was thought to be too imprecise for KS3 but evidence showed that a demand for an accuracy of 2mm would yield achievement levels approximating to the Science Working Group's predictions. In practice many of the trial and pilot SAT tasks were based on predictions of pupil performance. Subsequently, pupils' responses have provided exemplars which assist in the interpretation of criteria.

Developing SATs
When the agencies commissioned to prepare the first SAT materials began work there was no clear, universal understanding of what a SAT would look like. The invitation to tender document issued by the School Examinations and Assessment Council (SEAC, 1989) used a quotation from the TGAT Report and described SATs as 'packages of tasks administered through a range of modes'. First endeavours towards producing assessment materials for KS3 science SATs were concentrated on supporting good practice. Classroom tasks were designed which incorporated practical experiences and which would yield outcomes for assessment. As far as possible tasks were constructed with a diversity of modes of presentation (CATS, 1990). Adoption of TGAT's recommendation to provide a diversity of modes of pupil response proved to be much more difficult. Teachers, as we have already noted, were struggling with the plethora of SoAs and had little or no prior experience of assessment by criterion statements. It was obviously going to be unrealistic to expect teachers to carry out much by way of oral assessment as part of SAT assessment. Consequently tasks tended to be designed which gave a written outcome. Tasks were trialled that attempted to differentiate across levels by outcome. A second strategy involved a series of tasks each focused on a specific SoA or more often a single attribute of an SoA.

Generally it was found that, for profile component 2, differentiation by outcome did not work well. One reason for this has already been noted, namely the lack of continuity within the hierarchy of SoAs in an AT. The second factor was only revealed by the trials. If a question is asked in general terms, a pupil who is quite knowledgeable may respond with many correct statements but not hit on points that unequivocally show achievement of the specifics of an SoA. Differentiation by outcome relies upon a certain degree of openness which allows the respondent to show a little or much knowledge and understanding. In practice questions which gave this measure of freedom frequently led many pupils to write answers which missed any positive achievement against the criterion statements even though much of what they had written was accurate. Therefore SAT assessment of profile component 2 ATs moved in the direction of numerous short tasks, each targeting a particular SoA or even a single attribute. These tasks sometimes involved a short practical exercise but with a written outcome. Other tasks were presented by words or picture but sometimes the teacher was engaged in a class exercise which presented the task in context and then pupils made their individual written responses.

Generally the tasks were well received by pupils and teachers. They were perceived as appropriate curriculum activities. The quality of illustrations and the diversity of presentation were listed as positive features. Pupils were less enthusiastic about the writing involved if too many activities followed in a consecutive series of lessons.

Against this positive feedback there were substantial criticisms. Many tasks required only a short answer which could be quickly appraised by the class teacher. Even so, when a class of 30 pupils completed series of tasks, each designed to give a level in three or four ATs, the teacher faced a formidable volume of marking in a short intensive period.

A further issue generated concern in many places. It was soon learnt that time was wasted and pupils' motivation quickly lost if the assessment task was either too easy or too difficult. Yet SAT testing was expected to cover all KS3 pupils including those still working towards level 1 and those already achieving above level 7. With a bank of tasks, each designed for a specific SoA, economy of testing time could be achieved by putting tasks together in some sort of banding arrangement. In the 1991 pilot (CATS, 1991), three overlapping bands (levels 1 to 4, 4 to 6 and 6 to 8+) were found to work reasonably well. Indeed over 90 per cent of pupils had a spread of performance of three levels or less in the ATs in which they were assessed. This range of performance of individuals was consistent with that indicated by TA.

To some teachers totally committed to mixed ability teaching, allocation of pupils to bands was unacceptable. While they registered their protests most schools operated the banding system. The bottom band did provide means for many less able children to show positive achievement. The short tasks engaged these pupils and boosted their enthusiasm but attracted adverse media comments because, taken out of context, they were portrayed as trivial and demeaning for 14-year-olds. It was an almost inevitable consequence of the assessment by task approach that complaints of trivialization and of atomistic testing would arise. However it was not publicized that some level 8 tasks were regarded by teachers as being too difficult.

Exploration of science (AT1)

AT1 presented a particular set of problems to the SAT developers. Because AT1 formed a separate profile component, the SAT specification required that it be assessed. The summary statement which described AT1 signalled both its essential quality and complexity. Even at a glance the number of level statements was intimidating. Level 3 had no fewer than nine SoAs and level 4 had ten. Level 6 introduced the requirement for a pupil to 'contribute to the analysis and investigation of a collaborative exercise' and went on to specify numerous criteria which required discussion and consultation with other pupils. This obviously would present problems in a SAT! Clearly no single investigation would reveal a pupil's competence in more than a small selection of the SoAs and this meant that either each SoA had to be assessed by a specific task or an alternative 'broad brush' approach had to be devised. The latter was preferred because it was felt that the spirit of AT1 was best captured by a whole investigation rather than by measuring performance of atomistic skills; in other words, AT1 did lend itself to differentiation by outcome.

However, the work of the Assessment of Performance Unit (APU) (Black, 1990) found that, when carrying out investigations, pupils' performance is much influenced by context. Could one SAT investigation give a sufficiently reliable measure? Furthermore, the DES-funded Open-ended Work in Science Project (OPENS) (Simon, Jones, *et al.*, 1991) showed that only a minority of schools already engaged their KS3 pupils in investigations of the kind envisaged. With an awareness of these factors, but also drawing upon experience of the Graded Assessment in Science Project (GASP) (Swain, 1989), development work began to find pragmatic solutions to these problems.

A framework for investigations evolved which allowed pupils three to four hours of lesson time to complete their work. The task of motivating pupils was delegated to teachers who were supported by notes which gave guidance on possible contexts. Flexibility in choice of contexts was seen to be important so that local factors could be taken into account. In addition to setting the context it was sometimes necessary for pupils to have time to handle and become familiar with any apparatus they might need to use. This was especially important before the new curriculum had been fully implemented when the topic might fall outside pupils' previous experience. The sequence for these investigations became:

(1) teacher setting the context;
(2) pupil planning;
(3) performing the investigation; and
(4) writing a report with results and conclusion.

In their first encounter with SAT investigations, teachers' reactions were polarized into two camps. Some expressed pleasure at the holistic approach and proclaimed that they were already working in this way. The majority though were either hesitant or openly hostile about embarking into such unfamiliar territory. They voiced doubts about pupils being able to make plans and feared management problems if pupils planned along divergent lines so that several different things might be going on simultaneously in the laboratory. Concerns were voiced about pupils' ability to write accounts of their investigation when their normal practice was to complete tables and sentences at the end of a worksheet. These fears underlined the need for support for teachers before SAT delivery through INSET and teacher guide books. Equally they pointed to the importance of strong guidelines for pupils who were new to this approach. A pupil guide card was designed with a series of simple questions appropriate for each stage, planning, doing and reporting. This quickly proved to be effective in helping pupils to tackle the task successfully. Moreover feedback from pupils revealed their pleasure at being able to plan their own investigations. Over the two years of development and trialling, culminating in the 1991 pilot, teachers too seem to have lost their initial apprehension because questionnaire returns after the pilot showed a massive majority in support of this investigatory approach to AT1. One senior science adviser claimed that SAT investigations had accelerated a major beneficial change in the teaching of science.

Devising a scheme for awarding a level of attainment presented a further challenge. To match the sequence of a pupil's written account (planning, performing and concluding) the SoAs were grouped in three columns headed planning, implementing and concluding. When marking, teachers were instructed to identify in a pupil's account the highest SoA under the planning heading for which there was evidence of achievement. The same process was then repeated for both implementing and concluding. During trials various ways of aggregating these three SoA 'scores' were appraised. This scheme did find a way through the labyrinth of SoAs in AT1 but it involved teachers in lengthy periods of marking. The best way to arrive at a final AT level was still under discussion when a new AT1 structure and a new National Curriculum assessment regime was announced. Nevertheless progress has been made along lines that have received substantial teacher and pupil support but several research and development issues remain in need of further study. Assessment by teachers of ephemeral evidence from oral tests or through observation is the key to valid practical assessment. Helping teachers to make these assessments to a common standard requires much further work. In many practical sessions, management issues, including those pertinent to safety, dominate teachers' attention. Making time for assessment judgements is difficult enough but most science practicals are based on small group activities so that there is the further complication of identifying the contribution of an individual to the work of the group. Experience so far suggests that class sizes of 20 pupils or less and technician support to ensure reliable apparatus are prerequisites for the kind of engagement of teachers with their pupils that allows monitoring individual performance.

Assessment in special schools
That SATs should be developed for pupils of all abilities, including those with special educational needs (SEN), was a welcome feature of the National Curriculum arrangements. The acute time pressures of the SAT production and trialling programme meant that limited attention was given to the SEN dimension. Nevertheless several special schools made a valuable contribution to SAT development and perhaps it may be claimed that these SEN teachers were helped to find their way around the science curriculum 'wood'. As a result of their involvement, a number of general factors emerged that merit attention by LEAs, science teachers and those charged with future assessment arrangements.

Many special schools have no specialist science teacher and lack the facility of a laboratory with the customary range of apparatus. Inclusion of special schools in early SAT developments therefore presented some SEN teachers with an enormous challenge but also gave them an opportunity to develop their science programme. Their response was remarkably enthusiastic and participation helped them to feel included in the science teaching fraternity. Stimulation was given to science teaching in these schools and encouragement to borrow apparatus from neighbouring secondary schools further helped to erode SEN teachers' feelings of isolation. The SAT materials, with their emphasis on good practice, were eagerly received by teachers who were free to modify them for their pupils. Often the SAT tasks provided vehicles for science teaching that teachers themselves might not have thought of producing because of their non-science background. The flexibility of the tasks meant they could usually be accommodated within the integrated pattern of the school day. Yet, despite these positive features, SEN teachers were divided on the advisability of SATs for these pupils.

The negative dimensions of SATs for SEN pupils deserve consideration. Modification of a test task to make it accessible to a pupil with a particular need is often time consuming. The very act of modification may change the validity of the task and so further scrutiny of the revised task becomes essential. Many SEN pupils need support from an adult in order to access the task and, perhaps, to make a tangible response. In special schools this degree of adult support is generally available but SEN pupils in mainstream schools may not so readily receive the same measure of support. For these reasons teachers in special schools were most concerned about comparability of standards. The span of concentration of some SEN pupils is very limited and working to complete an assessment programme within a limited time slot proved difficult, especially for pupils whose emotional and behavioural characteristics account for their placement in a special school. For some pupils the written test may be inappropriate and, while it has to be recognized that adapting assessments for SEN pupils will be costly, there are sufficient positive features from this early work to justify the hope that the important entitlement dimension of the National Curriculum will ensure that further work is done in this area of assessment development.

Same 'wood', new 'trees' and new assessment

It is too early to evaluate the long-term contribution of the initial two years' work on assessment of National Curriculum science at KS3. Two contrasting avenues of development have been commissioned for the next phase. SAT packages as specified for the first writing contract have been superseded by three one-hour examinations for 1992. These 'pencil and paper' tests will give a measure of pupil performance across all the new ATs, excluding AT1. With fewer ATs and less SoAs the curriculum 'wood' appears smaller and more manageable but this is an illusion because the content covered in the programmes of study is little changed. To complement these examinations the writing agency has been asked to provide teacher and pupil support materials for a non-statutory SAT for AT1 together with supplementary TA materials for all other ATs.

These two different assessment activities are likely to have contrasting effects on the way teachers approach the curriculum. The examination papers will create pressure for teaching facts and principles that lend themselves to short, sharp testing. Conversely, TA support should encourage the further development of investigational practical science without the time constraints which the formal SAT imposed. Similarly, good support materials should help teachers gain confidence with a criterion-related form of assessment. If this happens then the goals of the TGAT Report may yet begin to be realized. Once teachers have become familiar with the curriculum map and have internalized diagnostic indicators of achievement at different levels, much routine classroom discourse will provide the alert, listening teacher with informal evidence of pupil achievement. These informal assessments will be amenable to formal verification by diverse laboratory and classroom activities. If this scenario develops, teacher-assessed levels of pupil performance will be informed by sound professional judgements. Such assessments should have high validity and the end of key stage examinations need then only serve as a means of standardization between teachers, schools and local authorities.

The alternative possibility is for TA to become devalued and for examination cramming to begin to threaten both the curriculum itself and pupils' enthusiasm long before they reach the horizons of KS4 and GCSE. Until the pattern of events becomes clear, the optimist will hope that the early developmental SAT work will prove to have begun to open up promising assessment paths through the 'wood' of National Curriculum science.

References

Black, P. J. (1990) 'APU Science – the past and the future.' *School Science Review*, Vol. 72, No. 258, pp. 13–28

CATS Science Team (1990) *Trial 1990: Final Report*. Submitted to SEAC but not published.

CATS Science Team (1991) *Pilot 1991: Report* and *Appendix*. Submitted to SEAC but not published.

DES (1985) *Science 5–16: A Statement of Policy*. London: HMSO.

DES (1988a) *Task Group on Assessment and Testing: A Report*. London: DES/WO.

DES (1988b) *National Curriculum Science for Ages 5 to 16*. London: HMSO.

DES (1989) *Science in the National Curriculum*. London: HMSO.

Essex LEA (1991) *Strands*.

SEAC (1989) *Development of Standard Assessment Tasks for pupils at the end of the third Key Stage of the National Curriculum.* London: School Examinations and Assessment Council.

Simon, S. A., Jones, A. T., *et al.* (1991) *Open-ended Work in Science: A Review of Existing Practice.* King's College London: Research Series No. 1.

Swain, J. R. L. (1989) 'The development of a framework for the assessment of process skills in a Graded Assessment in Science Project.' *International Journal of Science Education,* Vol. 11, No. 3, pp. 251–9.

Chapter Three
Assessing English at Key Stage 3: Dilemmas for SAT Developers

Gordon Stobart and Tony Burgess

Eclipsed by the controversies over mathematics and science, the assessment of National Curriculum English has so far received relatively little attention. The main reason for this may have been that the subject structure was broadly in line with the recommendations of the Task Group on Assessment and Testing (DES, 1988) and, in comparison to mathematics and science, appeared to be both manageable and sensible. This impression was largely the result of a common-sense profile component (PC) structure (Speaking and Listening; Reading; Writing) and of being restricted to five Attainment Targets (ATs).

Our intention in this chapter is to show that the assessment of English is far from straightforward and, particularly at Key Stages (KSs) 3 and 4, raises issues which will become increasingly pressing, particularly for those developing the Standard Assessment Tasks (SATs). Our argument is that the wide-ranging entitlement curriculum generates assessment ambiguities within ATs. The cost of the relatively simple PC/AT structure is that much of the complexity of the subject resides within the Statements of Attainment (SoAs) which make up each AT. The practical outcome of this is that the current SoAs cannot be used directly as assessment criteria. This results from both their generality and their complexity.

This has left those implementing National Curriculum English with a difficult dilemma; should they seek a more explicit definition of the performance required by an SoA, or use the SoAs as guidelines for a holistic judgement about the level a pupil has reached, or ignore some of the SoAs and concentrate on what can be more easily assessed?

Our concern here will be to show the issues the KS3 SAT developers had to face in working within the TGAT framework and to record some of the positive benefits that emerged. We do this to keep on record two years of development work which has been swept away by the political decision to replace SATs by short written tests. In doing so we would wish to pay tribute to the Consortium for Assessment and Testing in Schools (CATS) KS3 English team which developed materials for trial SATS in 1990 and 1991. Evidence from the well-received pilot SATs involving over 17,000 pupils in 1991 was not considered in that decision.

National Curriculum English

The English Working Party, like TGAT before it, assumed that National Curriculum assessment would involve making judgements based on a range of evidence drawn from different contexts. This was to be the case for both teacher assessment (TA) and for SATs, which were envisaged as extended classroom tasks (DES, 1989, para. 14.22) This assumption allowed the profile components to reflect the range of skills and experience which were held to be part of each language mode. What is currently being ignored in the move to short, timed written tests is that many of the SoAs are not easily amenable to this type of single occasion assessment. For example, the performance expected of any average 14-year-old in AT2 (Reading) at level 6 can be seen to encompass a great deal more than could be captured in a short test, as the requirements below demonstrate. Students have to:

(1) Read a range of fiction and poetry, explaining their preferences through talking and writing, with reference to details.
(2) Demonstrate, in talking and writing about literature, non-fiction and other texts that they are developing their own insights and can sustain them by reference to the text.
(3) Show in discussion or in writing that they can recognize whether subject matter in non-literary and media texts is presented as fact or opinion, identifying some of the ways in which the distinction can be made.
(4) Select from a range of reference materials, using appropriate methods to identify key points.
(5) Show in discussion of their reading an awareness that words can change in use and meaning over time and demonstrate some of the reasons why.

This involves the *breadth* of a pupil's reading, and the ability to *discuss* literature critically with others, explaining preferences and showing awareness of the writer's style and the use of information skills. The irony is that while these are best assessed through TA this is likely to play a diminishing role in assessment at KS3 and KS4.

It is against this background that we shall consider the assessment issues posed by the general nature of the 'criterion-referenced' SoAs. Having given these an airing we then tackle the implications for teachers and those developing the SATs.

SoAs: Assessment issues

SoAs as assessment criteria

The National Curriculum is often presented, particularly in political rhetoric, as a criterion-referenced system of assessment. Closer scrutiny of the content of the SoAs suggests that 'criterion-referenced' is being used in a very loose way. What is usually being referred to is the way in which performance is *pre-specified* in the SoAs so that a pupil will be credited with level 5 performance for successfully attaining the requirements at that level. However, this soon becomes meaningless if these statements are couched in such general terms that they are subject to significant variation in interpretation by those who use them, particularly given the massive effects of *context* on how well pupils perform (Cresswell and Houston, 1990).

The English Working Party had to make compromises in this respect. Not only are the SoAs very general, they are also often highly complex and require several different criteria to be met within a single SoA. For example, in Speaking and Listening at level 9 the first of the three SoAs reads:

> ...give a presentation expressing a personal point of view on a complex subject persuasively, cogently and clearly, integrating talk with writing and other media where appropriate, and respond to the presentation of others.

While this may be an excellent brief for teaching purposes, for assessment purposes this SoA is so complex that, in practice, holistic judgements will be made with a considerable 'norm-referenced' element – for example, because it is level 9, this would be the performance expected of a grade A GCSE pupil.

Progression through levels

The problem of generalized SoAs is compounded by their patchy development from level to level. Movement between levels often hinges on slight shifts in wording, or the use of comparatives. For example, progression in Writing (AT3) from level 5 to level 7 in the first of the five SoAs involves moving from:

> ...write in a variety of forms for a range of purposes and audiences, in ways which attempt to engage the interest of the reader. (5a)

through:

> ...write in a variety of forms for a range of purposes, presenting subject matter differently to suit the needs of specified known audiences and demonstrating the ability to sustain the interest of the reader. (6a)

to:

> ...write in a wider variety of forms, with commitment and a clear sense of purpose and awareness of audience, demonstrating an ability to anticipate the reader's response. (7a)

This example may also be used to demonstrate another concern, namely whether the progression is genuinely hierarchical. It strikes us that presenting material for a 'specified known audience' (level 6) may often be easier than for an unspecified 'range ... of audiences' (level 5) if these are in unfamiliar contexts.

These examples are intended to demonstrate that if English is 'criterion-referenced' it is so only in the loosest sense and in assessing English a great deal will rely on the way teachers and SAT developers both provide the context and interpret the responses.

Elusive strands
One of the features of English is the way in which the SoAs are organized as strands which run through some or all of the levels. Typically there are three to five strands in each AT. This makes good sense in terms of continuity but becomes problematic for assessment when a strand disappears at a particular level only to resurface several levels later. For example, in Speaking and Listening 'expressing a point of view' first appears at level 7, is still present at level 8 but is omitted at level 9 and reappears at level 10. Even more problematic for SAT developers are those SoAs which appear as part of a strand at one level only. In Speaking and Listening we calculate that there are six such strands. For example 'conveying a message' appears at level 3 only, and 'giving a detailed oral account of an event' is restricted to level 4.

One further twist to this is when a strand is repeated in identical form at the next level. For example in Reading, the 'range' strand at levels 8, 9 and 10 is identical:

...read a range of fiction, poetry, literary non-fiction and drama, including pre-20th century literature.

(At level 7, 'explaining their preferences through talking and writing with reference to detail' is appended to the same statement!) Once again this may not be difficult to interpret from a teaching point of view, and the Cox Report stressed the recursive nature of English. However, it does make assessment difficult, particularly if one acknowledges that context plays a vital role in how pupils perform.

Assessing and aggregating ATs

Arriving at AT levels
Given the complexity of the individual SoAs, we are still left with the issue of how the performances they specify are to be combined into a single AT level. This difficulty was acknowledged in the June 1989 English Proposals which suggested that averaging the levels achieved on each strand was inappropriate given that they were not intended to be equally weighted (DES, 1989, para. 14.30) and that the numbers of strands vary by level (ibid, para. 14.29). The Working Party's proposal was a particularly tough-minded one and would meet the most stringent 'mastery' demands of criterion referencing:

...We believe that a pupil's reported level of attainment within each attainment target should normally be the level at which he or she has achieved every strand. (para. 14.31)

This approach was immediately softened by allowing exceptional cases such as near-misses on one strand or when performance is affected by problems such as shyness (ibid, para. 14.33). The Working Party also acknowledged that this approach might depress the overall levels achieved in English relative to other subjects.

By September 1991 this issue had still not been resolved for KS3 and KS4. SAT developers have so far opted for holistic judgements by teachers which, like current GCSE examinations, will allow a good performance on one strand to compensate for a weaker one in another, rather than to allow the weakest performance to set the level, as in 'pure' criterion-referenced approaches. The fact that an increasingly restricted number of SoAs will be assessed in future SATs will further complicate matters. How will, for example, SAT levels for strands (a) and (d) be combined with TA of (a) to (e)? Indeed the whole issue of how TA and SAT levels will be reconciled is yet to be decided, though current political pressures suggest a 'SAT-preferred' model in which SAT/TA discrepancies are resolved in favour of the SAT level, even if this involves a lighter sampling of fewer SoAs.

Assessing KS3 English

Solutions to the problematic legacy bequeathed by the Working Party and by TGAT can be attempted along one of two possible lines. Either restrict the SoAs to be assessed by SAT or co-ordinate them within a set of more general criteria. A third possibility, which we do not develop here (but others may already be doing) is to rewrite the English Order.

The first two alternatives are, in theory, not mutually exclusive. In practice one or other has tended to predominate in the solutions developed at KS1 and KS3. Whichever is adopted entails correspondingly different resolutions to the related problems of SAT form and of the TA/SAT relationship. Distinguishing between these two alternatives provides a means of disentangling issues in National Curriculum assessment which have emerged during the phase of implementing arrangements in both Key Stages.

The KS1 model

Restricting the number of SoAs to be assessed and targeting these through the development of specific assessment tasks has, by and large, been favoured in the assessment model which has emerged at KS1. This solution reflects the breadth of assessment required from KS1 teachers across all three core subjects. However, some major difficulties are generated by it.

The phenomenon of the shrinking curriculum is one of these. Reducing subjects to be assessed has only been one aspect of this. Pruning within subjects, including English, has also been required. Since SoAs, in all subjects, have not been formulated in co-ordinated ways or in a sufficiently graduated sequence, SATs attempting to target specific SoAs face problems in covering a sufficient number.

Among the 'technical issues' which have come to light in trialling and piloting at KS1, 'coverage' has therefore been one of the most insistent. Another set of issues has derived from the multiplicity of discrete tasks and complexity of recording instruments which are required as a further consequence of adopting this solution. This set has been dubbed, in SEAC-speak, 'manageability', and has figured largely in the national debate about the early KS1 assessment programme.

It is important to grasp how fundamentally the assessment arrangements at other Key Stages were influenced by decisions taken about the assessment model at KS1. They were not, of course, decisions taken unilaterally by the KS1 development agencies. They followed from the Secretary of State's adoption of the TGAT model, together with the implications carried by this for the reports of the Working Parties, and from SEAC's interpretation of this model to the KS1 agencies.

Many of the issues in National Curriculum assessment have arisen against this background. For example, the time occupied by an assessment task is *not* the most important consideration in assessing manageability, though it becomes so if many tasks are necessary in the interests of coverage. But short tasks can be just as disruptive and difficult to use if they are not harmonized with classroom settings and normal teaching and learning arrangements. Nor need TA and SAT assessment be thought of as having different and potentially conflicting, rather than complementary, roles. The more specifically targeted SATs are, however, the more likely it is that a wedge will be driven between them.

The KS3 model

The legacy of the English Working Party and of TGAT has been met in a different way in assessing English at KS3. In many Year 9 English classrooms, it is possible to find pupils performing at almost any of the full range of National Curriculum levels. In assessing at the later Key Stages, then, the problem which predominates is how to make assessments over the ten curriculum levels within a single subject, rather than across subjects and for relatively fewer levels as at KS1. This difference in the assessment task confronting SAT developers has been one consideration leading towards a different interpretation of the assessment model at KS3. Another has been the influence of GCSE.

The GCSE experience of making assessments across grades has been instructive in several ways, as have the lessons learnt from combining course-work and timed examination. In GCSE, judgements about grades are made against a set of broad objectives with course-work and (in some modes) an examination both supplying evidence for these judgements.

An alternative model to targeting specific SoAs has been developed against this background by the KS3 agencies. In this one, SoAs are incorporated and co-ordinated within general criteria which are applied in progressively elaborated forms across all National Curriculum levels. Judgements are made against these criteria. But SoAs can also be used to refine allocation to particular levels. For example, in assessing Speaking and Listening, a decision can be made in allocating pupils to levels, by assessing them against the broad criterion:

> ...Take a constructive part in group discussion, understanding the views of others and contributing to the development of the discussion. (levels 5/6/7)

This judgement can be refined or doubts resolved through reference to the particular SoAs.

The construction of general criteria of this kind has enabled an intermediate assessment instrument to be developed which overcomes many of the initial difficulties of National Curriculum assessment. This instrument still grounds English assessment in the SoAs, but avoids the fragmentation which results from adopting them too straightforwardly as the targets to be examined by SATs. There has also been an additional advantage because, once such an instrument has been developed, it is capable of wider use. Ongoing TA, no less than SAT development, has been hampered by the legacy of SoAs provided by the Working Party. Developing broad criteria which co-ordinate SoAs has enabled judgements derived from SAT assessment and from TA to be brought coherently together.

This solution leaves more scope for judgement on the part of the teacher/assessor than in tasks specifically targeted on SoAs. However, it is arguable that this is actually advantageous to good assessment and, further, to improving National Curriculum assessment as a whole. What is necessary to a system which rests equally on TAs and on SATs (which are also teacher assessed) is the coherence and consensus of professional judgements about what counts as successful performance. It follows that it is important to permit circumstances in which judgements of this kind can be made and consensus developed. Creating narrowly conceived assessment tasks may shunt aside the development of judgement and may anyway disguise the extent to which judgement is involved.

With judgement, ensuring the adequacy of 'evidence' available is a further issue which requires attention in this model. In assessing abilities in language, the evidence of one occasion is rarely satisfactory, since minute changes of content and context can create considerable variation in a task, even if larger constraints (of function or audience, for example) are held constant. The simple question 'which SoAs can be covered?'

leaves unaddressed the question 'how much evidence is needed in order to decide whether a student is capable of performing at this level?' Given that it is possible to gain some evidence about most SoAs when they are co-ordinated in broad criteria, the extent and quality of evidence become critical issues.

Part of the answer lies in perceiving the complementary nature of different assessment occasions and in assuming that several may underlie any final judgements which are made. For there is no marked disparity in nature between judgements made by teachers in the course of SATs and judgements labelled TA and made on different occasions in the course of a year's work. Each set reflects evidence of different kinds. A final judgement, allocating a pupil to a curriculum level, will draw profitably on a range of occasions, including, among them, SATs.

The solution which has been developed at KS3 accommodates, then, the range of levels over which assessments must be made at this Key Stage, and addresses in a related way the problems of coverage and the TA/SAT relationship. There is a final advantage to be derived from developing broad criteria and assuming that final judgements are made on the complementary evidence of TA and SAT assessment. This is that no restrictions are placed on the development of SATs which harmonize with classroom processes. SATs can take the form of effective sequences of classroom work, within which assessment windows are provided. Many of the so-called problems of manageability are avoided by developing SATs which have this form.

This, in outline, has been the model for assessing English at KS3 which has been trialled and piloted over the last two years. While there have been some differences in the work of the two development agencies, both have agreed on the advisability of an intermediate assessment instrument. Their work has had much in common.

The CATS 3 English team, whose work we naturally know best, has experimented more fully with allowing freedom for teachers to vary materials and activities, according to local circumstances. Such experiments included, at an early stage, the idea of an 'open' SAT (as well as guided and specified ones), in which materials were left entirely to the teacher's discretion. Subsequently, less radical solutions were found, which permitted local variation without exacting the development of SATs of different kinds.

Another area of experimentation by the CATS 3 English team has been with longer or shorter sequences of work. As indicated earlier, the key component in the form of the SAT lies in ensuring a manageable assessment window. But this window need not be coterminous with the sequence of the work. It may well be that schools would find it more manageable to have longer sequences of work, with two or more periods of assessment identified within the sequence. Trying out five- and seven-week sequences of work has allowed information about this to be gathered.

Without going into detail here, all the evidence gathered from extensive pre-piloting in the summer of 1991 suggests that the solutions adopted to the problems of assessment at KS3 have been remarkably successful. The judgements returned and analysed as pupil performance data indicate a high level of correlation between TA and SAT assessment. Teachers have had high praise for the quality of the SAT materials. With few exceptions, they have also welcomed the broad criteria statements and described these as more useful in guiding assessments than the SoAs used simply on their own. The overwhelming majority of teachers sampled found the SATs manageable, and valid and reliable assessments possible to make.

As it stands, then, the work of the development agencies in English at KS3 has provided an alternative model to that which has emerged at KS1. At the pre-pilot, in 1991, successful assessments were made on 17,000 Year 9 pupils in a manner which drew together TA and SAT assessment and received the strong endorsement of participating teachers. It had been expected that the work would be further refined through piloting in 1992 and would gradually come to influence the debate on national policy.

The new specification for SATs at KS3 in 1991
In June 1991, without reference to the teachers undertaking the pre-pilot and without waiting for the reports of the agencies, a new specification for SATs at KS3 was prepared, requiring one and a half hour tests for reading and writing.

These written tests – one for reading, two for writing – reflect decisions made by the Secretary of State. In effect, though without formal announcement, the principles of the TGAT Report, on which KS3 developments had been based, were abandoned, together with their problems. Such requirements run directly contrary to the arguments for new forms of testing made by TGAT. Only with the greatest difficulty can they be regarded as compatible with the assumptions and content of National Curriculum English.

One consideration is whether such tests can yield sufficient evidence to form reliable judgements about performance, even in those SoAs which can be assessed in this form. However, many SoAs in English, whether in reading or writing, cannot be covered straightforwardly by a written test.

Either large parts of the ATs in Reading and Writing, as well as Speaking and Listening, must be left with TA, and the TA/SAT relationship aggregated in proportions which recognize this, or we shall see an alternative logic within the new arrangements. This will require a revision of National Curriculum English in the light of the new assessment arrangements. These matters will no doubt occupy the months ahead.

There are other wider issues about the purposes to be served by National Curriculum assessment which we have not considered here. What we have tried to show is that the problems of the TGAT and Working Party inheritance are considerable and that assessment would never be straightforward. However, what the KS3 agencies did offer were approaches which sought to make valid assessments of the full scope of National Curriculum English. What we may now witness is the shrinking of that curriculum into what can be assessed by shrunken SATs.

References

Cresswell, M. J. and Houston J. G. (1990) 'Assessment of the National Curriculum: Some fundamental considerations.' *Educational Review*, Vol. 43, No.1, pp. 63–78.

DES (1988) *Report of the Task Group on Assessment and Testing*. DES/Welsh Office.

DES (1989) *English for Ages 5 to 16, Proposals of the Secretary of State for Education and Science and the Secretary of State for Wales*. HMSO: London.

Chapter Four
Assessing Technology at Key Stage 1

Kay Stables

Introduction

This chapter discusses the issues relating to the assessment of technological capability that have arisen through the development of a range of
non-statutory Standard Assessment Tasks (SATs) for technology at Key
Stage 1 (KS1). These SATs have been designed to support teacher
assessment (TA) in this area of the curriculum. The developments
covered both areas of the foundation 'subject' of technology – Design &
Technology (D&T) and Information Technology (IT). Many assessment
issues are pertinent to both areas, some are specific to one. Both common
and specific issues are dealt with in what follows.

The decision made by the Secretaries of State that the assessment technology at KS1 should be based on TA is one that has been welcomed by
many in the education profession. However, its feasibility presupposes that
teachers of young children have an understanding and experience both of
the appropriate assessment skills and of the particular capabilities to be
identified within the spheres of IT and D&T.

At present this experience and understanding is generally patchy and
undeveloped. Aspects of technological activity in KS1 classrooms have
emerged through a variety of routes such as science and technology, art
and craft work, the use of computers and the introduction of versions of
the secondary CDT subject area. However, none of these fully embraces
the area of curriculum experience that is laid down in the National
Curriculum.

There is a good deal of concern over different aspects of technology
– areas where teachers lack confidence, terminology they are confused
by and so on. Feedback that was gathered from teachers involved in the
trialling of the technology SATs confirmed these concerns and indicated
lack of confidence both in planning and managing activities and in

making assessments. Teachers have not been used to making the more formalized assessments required by the National Curriculum; these are particularly complex in the areas of technology and demand assessment of procedural competence.

It is against this background of uncertainty that the development of National Curriculum assessment must be viewed. A measure of the success of its implementation will be the support it provides to increasing teachers' understanding and confidence, and to enhancing the development of children's capability in technology.

The need to develop valid and reliable assessment strategies
One main aim with National Curriculum assessment in general, and SAT development in particular, is to support teachers in making reliable judgements about the progress of children. Ensuring this reliability in technology is problematic for the following reasons:

- teachers working with this age group have little formal experience of the aspects of capability they are seeking to identify;
- the Statements of Attainment (SoAs) the teachers have to work from do not provide categoric exemplification of correct or incorrect evidence of achievement; and
- the Attainment Targets (ATs) and SoAs are fundamentally procedural – assessing process is complex and, as a profession, we have little experience of this type of assessment.

The root of these problems lies in the complex, procedural nature of valid technological activity. Attempting to ensure reliability while maintaining validity is hard work, but it can be seen how the two can be developed to support each other. One concern that is central to both is that of understanding. If teachers understand what they are looking at and what they are looking for there is more likelihood that they will assess that thing reliably. Similarly validity can only be achieved in technological activity if teachers understand the nature and purpose of the activity. Consequently a first principle in fostering both reliability and validity is to help teachers develop clear understandings, and a fundamental aim in SAT development was to achieve this in terms of both valid assessment and valid activity.

The importance of a holistic view
The development team was concerned to help teachers build and maintain a picture of a child's overall capability in D&T or IT. This position

was adopted partly because it is important in terms of technological capability and partly because it builds on the, possibly more tacit, assessment skills that most infant teachers already hold. Within this larger picture teachers also need strategies for assessing more specific aspects of capability that allow them to enhance their picture of the child and not fragment it.

Assessments can encompass everything from broad, overall judgements to those related to more detailed scrutiny. The experience of the Assessment of Performance Unit D&T team (Kimbell, *et al.*, 1991) indicated the importance of providing a framework in which assessments can be made, the surround of the frame relating to overall or holistic capability and, within the frame, groups of related aspects of capability. In National Curriculum technology, this framework can be seen to be structured by the profile components (PCs) as the surrounding frame with the ATs and SoAs providing a tighter focus on related aspects.

There are two contrasting approaches to managing this framework. On the one hand each aspect can be assessed as an isolated unit and the resulting judgements aggregated to produce an overall assessment. On the other, assessment can start with an overall assessment being made, related aspects then being assessed to provide a detailed picture of the characteristics of the overall judgement.

The ATs and SoAs in D&T have been written as an interrelated set of descriptors and exemplars that mesh together to characterize a holistic and integrated capability. Consequently, for D&T, the latter of the two options above was adopted as a more valid way of looking at the activity. It was felt that this approach was also important for reliability as individual statements become meaningless if divorced from those that surround them, making reliable assessment difficult.

For IT the picture is less clear as the links between a view of capability and the individual SoAs have not been made overtly. Also, individual SoAs can be viewed in a more discrete fashion and are more usefully looked at in terms of the strands that have been identified through non-statutory guidance (National Curriculum Council, 1990; Curriculum Council for Wales, 1990). However, holding an overall view of a child's capability has been shown to be important in order that the teacher can see how the child's achievements in a particular strand are contributing to a growing understanding of, and capability in, IT.

For these reasons, in the SAT trials assessment guidance for both D&T and IT was structured to assist teachers, first in making an overall professional judgement of a child's capability and then, using the ATs and SoAs, to look in more depth at the child's progress both to validate and inform the overall judgement and to diagnose individual strengths, weaknesses and needs for a particular child. Teachers were provided with criteria and guidance for making holistic or overall professional judgements of capability. However, there is some controversy over the appropriateness of this mode of assessment. Concerns have been expressed that it will lead to superficial and norm-referenced judgements being made. Despite this, it has been shown to be both a reliable and valid method in the APU survey (Kimbell, *et al.*, 1991) where the assessors shared both criteria and exemplar materials as guidance for making holistic assessment judgements. It also provides an approach welcomed by teachers involved in the SAT trials but, because it is seen as controversial, the use of holistic assessment remains in implicit form only in the SAT materials available directly to teachers. Explicit detailing of holistic assessment is, however, available in guidance to LEA advisers, its use with teachers being left to the discretion of individual LEAs.

The relationship between assessment activities and teaching and learning

The SAT materials do, however, indicate the value of using the SoA as a tool for diagnostic assessment to enable teachers to identify individual strengths and weaknesses in a child's way of working. Crucial to this has been helping the teacher to see the relationship between what is to be assessed, the intention within the technological activity, the nature of evidence and the way activities are planned.

In relation to the issue of matching assessment to intentions within the activity, the development team was concerned to ensure that, through the SAT, the teacher could see how the particular activities would give insights into the child's performance and, at the same time, structure valid and integrated technological activity. Throughout the development of the SATs there was a concern about the tension between meeting the needs of the teacher for deriving evidence of attainment and the needs of the child for involvement in valid activity. The danger of providing assessment strategies for the teacher that became mere hoop jumping exercises for the child was recognized as being all too great. In trying to make clear the relationship between the intentions in the processes of the activity and the assessment of attainment through the activity, it was hoped that teachers would be helped to become more aware of how assessment can be planned for, and go hand-in-hand with, the provision of creative learning opportunities for children. A further aim was to provide teachers with some criteria through which they could be more critical of activities that were of little or no benefit to the child. Figure 4.1 was used with teachers to help them see how these different aspects relate.

The activities built into the SATs were broadly of two types - those that relate to children taking action, such as making, exploring, modelling, organizing, controlling, and those that relate to children reflecting, both on the action already taken and on any they intend taking.

Both modes of working have been shown to be vital in technological activity (Kimbell, *et al.*, 1991) and both are important focuses for assessment – crudely speaking, the former gives insight into what children can do, the latter shows their understanding of what, why and how they are doing it.

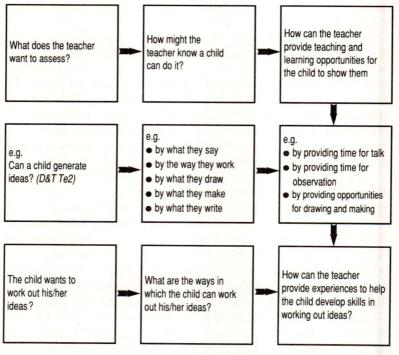

Figure 4.1 *The relationship between intentions in technological activity and assessment*

Looking for the 'spirit' of an SoA

Both the ATs and SoAs can be seen as providing characteristic descriptors of different aspects of a child's work and the SAT materials encourage teachers to use them in this way. However, teachers expressed concern that at times, even though a child's way of working indicated certain abilities, there was no tangible evidence of related statements being achieved. This highlighted a further issue in the assessment relating to the status of the SoAs: should they be seen as definitive and be applied 'to the letter', or should they be seen as the distillation of a particular characteristic of capability? Very often the problem the teachers encountered was to do with the wording of certain SoAs which appear to demand verbal or written comment from the child. For example, to attain AT4,3b the child must 'comment on the materials and processes used and how the task was tackled'. But is it the child's understanding of the materials and processes used and how they have gone about their task that is important, or their ability to comment? It was the view of the development team that while children need to develop an ability to comment on the processes they employ, the former is the more important in the development of capability. Consequently the SAT materials encourage teachers to look for what has been termed the 'spirit' of an SoA in order to separate out the underlying ability it is seeking from the vehicle that it suggests should provide the evidence. Once the underlying ability has been identified, the teacher can consider the appropriate forms the evidence might take. This is not to say that tangible evidence is not important. Indeed a major thrust in the development of capability is through the child increasingly being able to communicate both their actions and their reflection on their actions.

Developing shared understandings

It could be argued that such strategies only serve to produce more confusion through appearing to allow idiosyncratic interpretations of SoAs. In fact this strategy was employed to help teachers develop valid interpretations of SoAs in terms of promoting the development of capability and it would need to be supported by further strategies aimed at helping teachers come to shared understandings of levels of attainment. Two ways in which this can be done are being employed through the SAT developments. The first of these is the production of exemplification material that provides a set of examples of children's work representing a range of levels of attainment, a description of the context in which each took place and a commentary on the assessment judgements that were made. This material must be viewed carefully for it is at the same time potentially both useful and dangerous. The more concrete and explicit this exemplification is, the more useful it will be in terms of reliability. But there is a danger that it will indicate fixed responses or 'right' answers. However, it is hoped that teachers will use the exemplification materials to add to their own repertoire of appropriate responses to look for and not to provide prescribed outcomes to be taught.

A second strategy for developing common understandings is providing teachers with the opportunities to share experiences and discuss how children's work can be assessed. These opportunities are being promoted through 'agreement trials' set up within individual LEAs.

Using the SATs to enhance the curriculum

While the main aim within the development teams' brief was the development of valid and reliable assessment instruments, it was also seen as important that the SATs complemented good practice in infant classrooms and that the activities could be integrated into normal ways of working. At KS1 the teacher making an assessment of technological capability will at the same time be making assessments based on the core and other foundation curriculum areas as well as on other aspects of the child's development, such as social skills. For this reason topic-based approaches to curriculum planning were explored as vehicles that could be used for contextualizing a SAT. Teachers endorsed this as the most successful way to use the D&T SATs because it allowed them to draw in other areas of the curriculum and provide a rounded experience for the children. For IT it was seen as a crucial approach, as it allowed teachers to use the IT SATs to enhance work in a variety of curriculum areas rather than treating them as isolated experiences. The development teams were under constant pressure to see the curriculum role of the SATs as secondary. However, they felt a commitment to an assessment model in which assessment supports rather than leads the curriculum and consciously promoted the view that teaching and learning should take place alongside the SAT as many of the activities included both initiate and support learning. To deny that this happens (and, worse still, not to provide the learner with support at appropriate times) would be wasteful. This raised the issue of teacher intervention and the extent to which such intervention would invalidate the assessment. Consequently, teacher intervention in terms of the activity was seen not only as allowable but also desirable. However, in terms of the assessment, teachers were guided to assess only that which they were confident the child was able to do.

Research issues

The development of SATs has been tied very much to the principles behind the technology Order itself: for D&T, the importance of holistic activity, the interaction between the four ATs, the relationship between the imaging and modelling of ideas and of the importance of contextualized, purposeful activity; for IT, the importance of using IT to enhance activities across the curriculum and for children to develop understandings of how they can use IT and take a critical stance on where and when to use it appropriately.

In trialling the SATs, their practical application has been scrutinized, particularly in relation to the way they complement the ways in which young children learn. It has been important to focus on this because of the lack of research into developing both D&T and IT capability in the very young. While the fundamental nature of these capabilities pertains to all ages, historically the model for development has been created and explored by looking at adults and older children.

There is much similarity in the approaches to the development of technological capability and the learning of young children, but as yet there is no significant research to draw on. The appropriateness of technological activities needs to be considered in order to ensure that learning is consolidated, not fragmented. The SATs were trialled with a wide range of children; boys and girls, those in the nursery to those in Year 4, children with a variety of special educational needs, children not fluent in English, children from different cultural backgrounds. In general terms teachers found that the SATs were flexible enough to be used 'successfully' with all of these groups. But, on an individual basis, were each child's assessment needs being met? The SATs, for example, indicated gender differences in the performance data. What strategies should be employed to develop capability in both boys and girls?

The appropriateness of the SoAs became a further area of concern. Again in general terms, the SoAs appeared to produce a useful and appropriate set of descriptors, but anomalies began to emerge. Why, for example, is there no SoA that considers a child's ability to reflect on the use of IT until level 3? Is this based on research data or an assumption that young children don't reflect? Experience from the SAT trials would indicate that the lack of SoAs at levels 1 and 2 is wrongly founded.

The development of the SATs was not primarily set up to look at these areas, but inevitably the team looked at emerging pictures. Unfortunately the development raised more questions in terms of research than it answered, but what has been highlighted is the need for further and detailed research into this area of the curriculum in order that capability can be fostered through informed insights rather than assumptions.

Conclusion

The SATs are now available for use by any teacher who so chooses. Teachers who used them in trials generally endorsed the SATs as providing good classroom activities that helped the teachers develop insights into technological activities and focus on assessment in a way that allowed both overall judgements and a detailed scrutiny to be made, and provided children with motivating and challenging activities.

The success of the SATs on the 'open market' is yet to be ascertained, but it will depend very much on the extent to which teachers are provided with opportunities to explore the SATs' potential, for example through INSET sessions. Some measure of their value will be provided through the evaluation and monitoring of their introduction, on behalf of SEAC, by the Centre for Formative Assessment at the University of Manchester.

At an LEA level, the SATs have been well received as materials that provide classroom activities that will develop the technological curriculum at KS1 and at the same time enhance other areas of the curriculum. But concerns are already being expressed for KS2. It is to be hoped that these constructive developments in the foundation years will be built on to provide a structure for progression that will allow the technological capability of all children to flourish.

References

Curriculum Council for Wales (CCW) (1990) *Non-statutory Guidance for Design and Technology and Information Technology*. CCW.

Kimbell, R., Stables, K., Wheeler, T., Wozniak, A. and Kelly, A. V.(1991) *The assessment of performance in design and technology*. SEAC.

National Curriculum Council (NCC) (1990) *Non-statutory Guidance for Design and Technology and Information Technology*. NCC.

Chapter Five
Developing SATs for 7-year-olds

Shirley Clarke

Introduction

The term Standard Assessment Task (SAT) raises strong emotions in many infant teachers and may elicit words of anger and frustration. There have been 'expert' and media accounts of the SAT experience but little from the teachers who actually carried out the SATs or those who worked to develop them. In this chapter I will attempt to convey the reality of being a SAT developer for the Consortium for Assessment and Testing in Schools (CATS) from my experience of writing the SATs for the informal trials of 1989 and the pilot study of 1990, and working with teachers and listening to their comments about the experience.

The story began in January 1989, when three consortia were contracted to develop SATs: CATS, based at the Institute of Education, the National Foundation for Educational Research (NFER) with Bishop Grosseteste College from Lincoln and Standard Testing and Assessment Implementation Research (STAIR) in Manchester. Informal trials were to take place in 1989, followed by a national pilot in 1990. After this, one of the three agencies (the most 'successful') would win a contract to write the 'real' SAT for 1991. The brief from the School Examinations and Assessment Council (SEAC) was to: define a SAT; cover all the Attainment Targets (ATs) for the three core subjects of English, mathematics and science; and make it easy to administer, reliable and valid.

Knowing 7-year-olds, and the history of 'teaching to the test', the CATS team took the following stance, in accordance with TGAT's recommendations (DES, 1988):

- The SAT would be cross-curricular, activity based and unthreatening to children, in order to maximize opportunities for demonstrating achievement.

- The SAT would resemble good practice, even if it could not be a model of good practice in itself because of the constraints of the 'test'.
- Wherever possible, differentiation would be by outcome – that is, achievement would be assessed on the basis of the level at which a child 'performed', given an open-ended task.

We conducted a survey of teachers' expectations of SATs and found that they feared 'paper and pencil' tests, dominance of the timetable and negative curriculum backwash, so we seemed to be heading in the right direction for children and teachers at least. There was nothing we could do, however, about the general feeling of disquiet about the imposition of the SATs and the worry teachers expressed about the effect of 'labelling' children at such a young age.

The 1989 informal trials
The first SAT developed by the CATS team consisted of six activities, loosely linked by the theme of 'the environment'. Three of the activities are outlined briefly to give a flavour.

People who help us in school (Activity 1)
A visitor to the class talks about his/her job. Children draw and write about the visitor, collect information about favourite jobs and represent it graphically, write a letter of thanks and make an envelope for the letter.

The Ramp (Activity 2)
Given a ramp, a truck and three different loads, children in pairs discover how to make the truck go the furthest. They represent this freely, then in a structured form, then interpret a graph.

Growing Cress (Activity 3)
Cress is grown in four conditions: light, dark, wet and dry. Children write about this, keep a diary and answer questions.

There was always a tension between coverage and duration – the greater the coverage, the longer the activity would take to administer – so we sampled the ATs by trying to include assessment of at least one Statement of Attainment (SoA) from each of the first three levels. We were worried about imposing our interpretations of the SoAs at this stage, so left the teacher to interpret performance and to decide on the level of achievement. The primary aim of the informal trials was to establish the validity and reliability of this type of test, rather than to explore issues of classroom management although, inevitably, the feedback included this.

We asked teachers to decide what level children were at on the basis of their own teacher assessment (TA) at the beginning of the SAT and to record SAT results on optical mark read (OMR) forms for speed of analysis. They also had to highlight those SoAs achieved for each child during the SAT administration.

It was clear that administration was going to be a problem. Filling in the forms was time consuming and teachers felt that they were being cast in the role of an unpaid clerical assistant. They were in any event uneasy about deciding a level for each child so early in the child's school career and felt that the SAT should be administered later in the term.

Even though teachers were asked to trial only three activities with ten children, there were reports of how time consuming they were to administer. Teachers found it understandably difficult to simultaneously explain tasks, make observations and concentrate on children's responses to questions. At the same time they had to read the corresponding SoAs and make judgements about achievement; all this with the usual interruptions that are found in any infant classroom.

Teachers generally thought of the activities as providing good curriculum material, and many used them as starting points for further exploration. However, there were requests that the SAT activities should be more coherently linked and comments that it was not effective to run them alongside an existing class topic, as children kept wanting to know when they could return to their 'real work'. Teachers also said that the activities were so rich in outcome potential (i.e. they could identify achievement of many SoAs within one context) that we should include assessment of more SoAs; not to seemed a waste of an opportunity once everything was up and running. In the light of this feedback, the construction of the SAT activities themselves needed a total rethink.

When children work together on a task, it causes problems of reliability if you want to question children individually and be sure that the reply represents their own thinking (i.e. that the same task could be set up at another time and produce different results). Wherever more than one question had to be asked of children at the end of an activity, as in Activity 3, children began queueing to see the teacher, and then witnessed the questioning of another child.

I will describe the main findings of the 'growing cress' activity (Activity 3) to indicate the difficulty in designing tasks which are both reliable and valid.

(1) The teacher first invited children, as a class, to predict what it is that seeds need to grow. As many children obviously knew already, there

was general rebellion when the teacher then had to dictate that all children would be setting cress up in various conditions to find out. Many children did not do their best work as a result of this.

(2)   To involve all children and heighten the purpose, each child was asked to set up a saucer of cress for *one* of the conditions. This resulted in children taking ownership of 'their' saucer, and thus focusing on the development of one sample of cress rather than comparing all four. It also encouraged a competitive streak, with children's diaries reporting that 'mine is the winner'. Children who were unfortunate enough to have set up the saucer of cress to be grown in the dark without water were distressed and mutinous.

(3)   Children had to complete a daily diary. This was time consuming, and by the end of the week many children were bored and needed coaxing to write or draw. We subsequently amended our interpretation of a diary, to be an account which is kept at regular intervals, not necessarily every day.

(4)   When asked at the end of the activity 'what do plants need to grow well?', many children said water and dark, because, although spindly and yellow, that cress had grown the tallest. This reply resulted in failure to achieve the related SoA.

(5)   When asked to point out the root, stem and leaf of some cress, many children failed to do this with such a tiny specimen. Teachers believed that with a larger plant children would have achieved the SoA.

(6)   Children were asked 'what happens when we plant seeds in the garden?' This was to be assessed according to the child's reply, at level 1, 2 or 3 of maths AT14 which assesses probability. Level 1 would be either 'they grow' or 'they do not grow', level 2 would be 'they might grow' or 'they might not' and level 3 would be an answer which specified conditions and possibilities. In the event, the most 'sophisticated' children (those of a general level 3 standard) cut through the possibilities and gave one reply, 'they grow', thus achieving level 1 only.

These findings point to issues of context dominating and steering possible outcomes (such as the ownership taken of the saucers leading to a limited view of the experiment), the unpredictable nature of activity-based assessment, the effect of purpose on performance and the vast range of interpretation, both of SoAs and pupil performance.

Differences of interpretation appeared in various forms. The Teachers' Notes were often interpreted differently, resulting in non-standard treatment of the tasks. For example, resource instructions for 'the ramp' (Activity 2) specified 'an open-topped, freewheeling, rectangular conveyance with wheels that turn, that fits on the ramp'. Different interpretations meant that the size of the vehicle varied, and larger trucks went too far, causing the whole activity to be moved to a school corridor. That the truck could be of any design was also assumed, so more unstable vehicles would not travel in a straight line, therefore affecting the assessment of measuring. Articulated trucks only turned sharply, invariably crashing into walls and making the investigation impossible. Teachers also interpreted the SoAs in their own ways, especially if there was ambiguity in the statement. 'Produce, independently, pieces of writing using complete sentences, mainly demarcated with capital letters and full stops or question marks' (En 3/2a) caused enormous problems in interpretation. As failure to achieve this SoA meant a child would be assessed as level 1 rather than 2 or 3, many teachers ignored it, giving the 'best' writers in the class level 3, regardless of evidence of capital letters and full stops in their writing. This tendency to norm reference through ranking is still evident, and is not helped by the ambiguity and unspecified sophistication level of many SoAs. 'Use materials provided for a task' (MA1/1a), for example, could mean at the level of a toddler building with bricks or a 16-year-old using a calculator to solve a geometric problem. Old habits die hard, and teachers have norm referenced for years, so it is not really surprising that it is still taking place. In fact, as a result of the unclear SoAs, more teachers, it seems, are looking for 'levelness' by comparing pupils' performances.

Teachers requested more guidance in the interpretation of the SoAs in the pilot SATs. We realized we would have to define precise criteria for attainment, which in itself would cause problems since, by restricting the outcome, children might be disadvantaged if they gave an alternative but still valid answer.

The intervention made by teachers during SAT assessment was very varied, ranging from leading questioning or constant rewording, to short, sharp objective questioning. Teachers wanted their children to do well, and were particularly anxious when a child was not performing well in the SAT context, but were certain he or she 'knew' the answer. At post-SAT meetings, teachers expressed their concern over the non-standard nature of the assessments in this respect and requested that some kind of moderation be put in place to ensure that there was uniformity in the handling of the SATs.

Speaking and Listening was voted by teachers as impossible to assess by SAT because of the significance of the context. It was reported that children often did not speak, simply because they were not interested in the subject matter.

The issue of assessing bilingual children began to grow when we saw from our quantitative feedback that there was a pattern of bilingual children tending to perform less well on average than English-speaking children, according to TA (teachers' ongoing assessment levels). Also, these children tended to perform at higher levels in the SAT activities than their TA levels had suggested. The use of bilingual support teachers in administering the SAT meant that children were given a better chance in the trials to demonstrate their abilities by using their home language. Many teachers, however, do not have access to mother-tongue support, and this unfairness has been the cause of much bitterness over the past two years. The problem is that there is no realistic solution – do you make it 'fair' to all bilingual children by withdrawing all mother-tongue support, or make it fairer for some by allowing support where it exists? Issues like this exasperate teachers, who are generally extremely accommodating if something is perceived to be fair and worth while. Of course, discrepancies in TA and SAT scores are also caused by low teacher expectation. The SAT experience could be used positively to heighten teacher awareness, and examination of the factors in schools where discrepancies do not exist could lead to more valuable INSET in the future.

To summarize, teachers found the activities time consuming but fairly worth while as curriculum material. There were many cases of unreliability, differences in interpretation and varied teacher intervention. Teachers nevertheless preferred this approach to more formal methods of assessment, but wanted more assessment per task and a more coherent package. Positive feedback included: increased assessment expertise, more familiarity with SoAs, opportunity to work collaboratively with colleagues, identification of gaps in practice and curriculum and a feeling of knowing the ten children better than the others.

The 1990 pilot

In the summer of 1990, two pilot SATs were trialled by the CATS team, this time with *all* children of Year 2 age (mostly six years old), in 20 LEAs throughout the country using ten to 12 schools in each LEA. Taking the 1989 feedback into consideration, and recommendations by SEAC, the SATs were restyled in the following ways.

- A SAT consisted of eight activities, linked by the theme of 'change' or 'movement', which could be chosen by the LEA.
- Each activity consisted of distinct parts, including non-assessed parts which provided context and purpose.

- ATs were sampled as before, but specific interpretations or 'evidence of attainment' of each were outlined, in the context of the particular task.
- Strategies were given to combat copying, such as pairing and grouping arrrangements and alternative questioning and timing.
- All children did the tasks from level 1 to level 3, to give maximum opportunities for achievement. The tasks were resource based and open ended, so it was perceived that all children would be able to operate at their own level and achieve something worth while for each task, regardless of its level.
- The teacher instructions were much fuller and included precise wording of questions for assessment in order to make this more standard and reliable.
- The reading assessment was focused around an unseen text (a book which we had written and illustrated) which could be used for children at all three levels.
- Speaking and Listening assessments were included wherever appropriate rather than as a separate assessment, giving teachers a range of contexts so that children were not disadvantaged by having only a single context in which to assess.
- Teachers were again asked to complete OMR forms for both TA and SAT scores, as there was no alternative method available.
- 'Milestone maps' were produced, indicating how the activities could be introduced and spread over a three-week period.

Observations and feedback

The findings of the 1990 pilot indicated that the small problems of 1989 had exploded, new problems had emerged and much of the teachers' optimism which we had conveyed in our training was fast disappearing down a cynical chute. Teachers found the experience exhausting; there was far too much assessment to be done, it was only really possible with another teacher in the classroom to enable individual questioning to take place, and teachers were having to spend hours after school either recording results, planning the next day or reading and learning the activities. What is more, they felt that they had learnt nothing really new about the children. The idea of using the SAT activity as a starting point for further exploration, as in the informal trials, was never mentioned again. Teachers were having to spend every minute of the day on 'SATting' in order simply to finish. The most positive feedback came from those teachers who received mental and physical support from the head and those who were used to talking to and working with children as individuals and who had decided to attack the SATs positively with an attitude of 'I'll do what I can and no more'.

Perversely, one of the biggest problems was the high level of professionalism teachers displayed, and were not given enough credit for: no matter how clear it seemed that the activities would *not* fit into a three-week period, many teachers believed that there might be a teacher nearby who was finding the whole thing manageable, and so strove to achieve what was practically impossible. The 'milestone maps' did not help the situation because they seemed to be saying that it was indeed possible in the given time. The new, coherent SAT package proved to be a failure for many teachers. Although they believed a topic-based SAT would be an improvement, the reality was that it dominated everything and left no space to do alternative work. Teachers decided that a subject-specific SAT would be more manageable because it would slot more easily into lessons.

Ironically, many teachers admitted that the children actually enjoyed the SAT activities, perhaps because of clearer purposes and targets, higher expectation of performance and the increased attention from their teacher. Where behaviour deteriorated or children were anxious, it tended to be as a result of the stress felt and conveyed by the teacher, and the lack of contact due to the style of administration of the SAT.

The more specific criteria for attainment now provided for teachers seemed a positive move, but inevitably they too had to be interpreted. This was particularly problematic in the more 'process' style SoAs.

The constraint of a theme (for example, having to make all SoAs fit a context of 'movement') caused some of our writing to be obviously 'tacked on' in order to achieve coverage. This led to differences in results between the two themes. Context differences were apparent in many places as a result of running two parallel SATs. For example, in 'change' children found it harder to talk about 'pushing and pulling' in relation to the movement of their bodies than in 'movement', where this was set in the context of steering a vehicle with a magnet.

The idea that the more able children could successfully work through all three levels was generally disputed by teachers. To begin with, this needlessly increased the amount of time spent on assessment. Secondly, children communicated the fact that they were being given work that was too easy for them (for example, ordering four one-digit numbers (3, 5, 1 and 7) for a level 1 maths task) or were clearly having difficulty with tasks which were beyond them. These findings were also discovered by the other two development agencies (NFER and STAIR), and led to the

SEAC specification for the 1991 SAT requiring provision to be made for 'exit' and 'entry' points, to be determined by the teacher. Although teachers had asked for more detailed guidance, the new, fuller version proved to be too unwieldy. We finally realized that it was clearer guidance they needed, not more of it.

The 'scripted' questions proved to be difficult for teachers to adhere to and felt unnatural, so that children were disadvantaged by not having their teacher phrase a question in his/her usual way. This is a typical 'no win' situation, where the more reliable the test, the less valid it can become. Teachers were also increasingly more aware of the dilemmas of this kind in assessment procedures, a fact demonstrated in the post-trial meetings we held. In these informal feedback sessions, teachers expressed frustration over the realization that the aspects of the SATs they did not like were the very aspects which made them standard and reasonably reliable – for instance, basing the assessment on the SoAs, presenting occasional resource sheets, asking teachers to set up an activity in a specific way, scripting some questions and dictating resources to be used.

Varied teacher intervention continued to be a factor in the reliability of the SAT, but with added anxiety on the part of many teachers. After our training sessions, where we showed videos of 'leading' and 'non-leading' intervention, many teachers were confused, and lost confidence in their ability to 'say the right thing'.

The reading assessment was heralded by many as a revolutionary way of assessing children as readers providing a full, diagnostic, formative and summative record. However, the content and presentation of our home-made books was rightly heavily criticized. The assessment was very time consuming, but worth while and, for many teachers, provided an introduction to strategies such as using a running record to assess a child's reading aloud (a strategy continued in 1991 and 1992). I believe that dropping the reading assessment using an unseen text in the 1991 SAT was misguided, as the exercise lost its element of standardization, and this was probably a major factor in the decision to include a written reading test in the 1992 SAT.

Teachers' initial reaction, that we should maximize each assessment opportunity by the inclusion of more SoAs, changed when the reality of trying to remember so many SoAs at once made them realize it would not work. In one case, we had no less than 21 SoAs for a teacher to focus on in one context (increased by all the possible Speaking and Listening SoAs), which was clearly unmanageable. But it was not until teachers had actually tried out many of their own suggestions that they realized they preferred the approach in the original trial SATs. Speaking and Listening itself was again seen to be very difficult to assess confidently, and proved to be time consuming. As a result of similar feedback from the other agencies, Speaking and Listening was excluded from the 1991 SAT, a decision not made easily, as it is an area of the curriculum which would benefit from high status treatment.

The administration demands were probably the last straw for many teachers. Completion of the OMR forms for a class of 30 children could take anything from four to 17 hours, and there were accounts of head-teachers taking the whole school while all teachers helped out, and of teachers needing release time to complete them or having to spend hours of their own time at home.

The use of the pilot SAT in six varied special schools in Birmingham produced results similar to those thrown up by analysis of the data concerning bilingual children. Although bilingual and special needs issues are of course completely separate from one another, our data showed that there are similarities between the two concerning teacher under-expectation and pleasant surprises about the children's perform-ance in this sort of assessment situation.

Teachers in certain LEAs were fortunate enough to have a bilingual support teacher to administer the SAT in the child's home language. In many cases of this kind, especially for science, there were discrepancies between TA and SAT results, with the SAT result nearly always being higher. Even when the class teacher administered the SAT, bilingual children often achieved higher levels than the teacher expected. These findings raise questions about expectation, access to the curriculum and effective use of mother-tongue support, one of the more constructive and helpful aspects of SAT research.

The positive outcomes of the pilot SAT were similar to those from the 1989 trials, with the added benefit that many teachers felt clearer about interpreting the SoAs and planning their ongoing assessment programmes with more confidence. Some LEA advisers and inspectors reported some positive changes in classroom practice, such as teachers beginning to provide for collaborative work, making use of resources more readily and feeling more confident with investigative work, where previously this had seemed too daunting.

After the media treatment of the pilot, it seemed that SEAC had finally realized that coverage of all of the ATs was not possible. Unfortunately, the furore over unmanageability drives those in power increasingly nearer to a *manageable* 'paper and pencil' test, something which, even during the worst moments of the SAT development programme, the majority of our teachers still resisted.

References

DES (1988) *National Curriculum Task Group on Assessment and Testing: A Report*. Department of Education and Science and Welsh Office.

Chapter Six
National Assessment at 7: Some Emerging Themes

Caroline Gipps, Bet McCallum, Shelley McAlister and Margaret Brown

Introduction

This chapter builds on the work of our ESRC[1]-funded research project *National Assessment in Primary Schools: An Evaluation.* This is an independent study of the introduction of national assessment at primary level, monitoring the implementation of the assessment system and the interpretation and use of results. Through focusing on teachers' developing assessment practice and the articulation of the national assessment model we aim to extend the theoretical frameworks of assessment; specifically we intend to further our understandings of the requirements for criterion-referenced assessment systems, the shifts in our perspectives on reliability and validity in new forms of assessment, and the relationship between assessment used for formative purposes and for summative/evaluative purposes.

The study involves in-depth work with teachers using detailed discussion, interview and observation in a range of primary schools. We have based our study in four LEAs, which were chosen to represent a range of different settings both socio-economic and physical: a north-eastern county, a south-eastern shire, a London borough and a midlands metropolitan borough. Both of the last two have considerable numbers of pupils whose first language is not English. Within each LEA we have chosen a stratified random sample of eight schools. We visited each school in the spring term of 1991 to discuss their experience of teacher assessment (TA). In the summer term we revisited each school; we

---

1   Ref: R 000 23 2192

observed the Year 2 teacher giving Standard Assessment Tasks (SATs) and we again interviewed the teacher and head in relation to this phase of national assessment.

This chapter is based on our summer 1991 school visits and addresses issues in relation to the administration of the SATs in 1991. It does not include our analysis of TA or a full account of the LEA setting and provision of support for SATs and TA. This will be presented in later accounts. First we shall present some of the findings, then we shall comment on the analytic themes which are emerging, finally we offer a critical commentary.

Changes brought about to support the SAT experience

School organization

Many primary schools made some changes to their organization in order to support the Y2 teacher.

Of our 32 schools, only ten had classes made up entirely of Y2 children; two had team teaching with Y1 and Y2 children together; the rest had mixed age classes or other forms of team teaching. In only seven schools was 'our' Y2 teacher the only Y2 teacher. The number of teachers involved in SATs in our schools ranged from one to five, with all the staff being involved in one first school. Clearly the task for a sole Y2 teacher, or a teacher with 25 to 30 Y2 children in his/her class, is very different from that for a teacher in a school where two or more staff each have eight to 12 Y2 children to assess.

Schools, not surprisingly, varied in the amount and type of changes which they made to support their teachers. Some were barely affected, with very few changes made to accommodate SATs. At the other extreme were the schools which reported total disruption, involving shunting staff around, re-timetabling the school day, cancelling meetings and activities and re-allocating space and resources. In one school virtually nothing remained unchanged:

The reception/Y1 teacher leaves her own class to do all the reading SATs on three mornings per week while the nursery teacher takes the reception class and two nursery nurses look after the nursery. Any parents who want to help are put in reception; the reception's full-time auxiliary is put into one Y2 class while another auxiliary, who normally works with a statemented child, is moved to the other Y2 class. Classes are doubled up for story time and assembly has been changed from mid-morning to first thing. INSET attendance and curriculum development meetings are stopped and teachers other than Y2 take on more assembly and playground duties. The head, as a moderator, is out of school for up to 22 days with no supply cover available. *(Field notes)*

Teaching and ancillary support offered

Two of our LEAs made some provision to support schools and teachers over the SATs period. In one LEA support teachers were provided if heads requested it in writing: six of the eight schools in our sample from that LEA had support teachers for times varying from two days in total to three days per week over the SAT period. In another LEA, a day's supply cover was available and 10 hours of ancillary help was also given to each school, regardless of size. Larger schools saw this as unfair. The other two LEAs did not appear to offer the same formal arrangements for support, although other kinds of LEA support were offered.

In most cases of teaching support, cover was provided for the class by a supply, support or headteacher while teachers carried out SATs in another room or in a private area within the classroom. In some cases the class was moved to another room while the teacher and the SATs children remained, or the various staff worked alongside each other. The number of adults in a classroom varied: in 17 classrooms where the whole class was present during the observation, nine classes had at least two adults present, five schools had three adults, and only two schools had one adult coping with the whole class alone while administering SATs. In one school there were four adults in the classroom: a teacher, an ancillary, a parent and a student on work experience.

Support was sometimes used to provide the teacher with non-contact time before, during or after the SATs period. In some cases planning was done before the SAT period with the support teacher; in other cases support was given after SATs to provide teachers with time to do their record keeping. Two schools kept support after SATs for the purpose of 'settling things down': one full-time ancillary was kept in the Y2 class for two weeks after SATs in order to help the teacher 'get her class settled down and back to normal' after the trauma of SATs.

In seven cases SATs themselves were carried out by someone other than the child's own teacher. Usually, this involved the child reading to the head (especially for level 3 reading), but in one situation the science SAT was carried out by the school's part-time science teacher and all the reading SATs were done by the special needs teacher. In a school where one of the Y2 teachers was absent a support teacher carried out all maths and science SATs for all the Y2 children while the head did reading. And in another case, the Y2 teacher, although present throughout SATs, did only English and a bit of maths while a supply teacher did all the science and the rest of the maths assessment.

In one school where teachers work in teams, one Y2 teacher did all the maths SATs for all Y2 children and the other Y2 teacher did all the science SATs: children did English SATs with their own teachers. In another team teaching situation, one teacher withdrew four children for a SAT while his colleague and a supply teacher shared the teaching of 64 children in an adjoining room.

In a few schools parents were planned into school organization and were seen to play an important part in the provision of support during SATs. One school sent a letter to parents explaining about the disruption in school caused by SATs and parents responded by 'volunteering in floods'. We observed parents in class in five schools. Indeed, there was one parent who, together with an educational assistant, was in charge of all non-SAT children, although with the teacher still in the same room.

Support by heads

Five heads were moderators for the LEA. This in itself was sometimes seen as support because information and advice were readily available to be filtered down to the Y2 teacher. On the other hand, heads who were moderators were out of their own schools much of the time and may have been unavailable to offer active support in the same way as non-moderating heads.

In half of the 32 schools, heads took an active role: six took classes while teachers administered SATs in another room; five carried out some or all of the reading SATs themselves, usually at level three, which is the most time-consuming; and one was observed doing a science SAT. Other heads helped out in classrooms for a set period each week, or contributed support by taking more assemblies or dealing with equipment.

In the 16 schools where heads did not get actively involved (for example, because of moderation or teaching duties), support from other quarters was usually provided. In most of these schools teachers worked in informal teams of three or four and were assumed to support each other. In fact they did: in five of the schools with some form of team teaching, Y2 teachers reported 'good collegial support' and seemed to derive mutual support and satisfaction from working together. In three schools Y2 teachers who did not normally work in teams had refused 'help' from their colleagues, although the nature of this help was not clear. The seven teachers who were the only Y2 teachers in their school often received sympathy, rather than practical help, from their colleagues.

In only one school did the head not offer *any* kind of teaching support or non-contact time during the SAT period although moral support was clearly available to the Y2 teacher. High support was often provided to protect teachers who were vulnerable, while low levels of support were likely to be related to school organization. Support often involved buying in expensive teaching support and/or causing disruption to the school by shunting staff into Y2 classrooms. Heads varied not only in the amount of support they offered but also in their attitude towards 'making SATs work'. One head refused to put in support. She felt that SATs should be workable for professionals in a natural situation and should not need the artificial and expensive support so many heads were offering; this was said in the context of a competent and experienced teacher, with only eight Y2 children to be tested. There were also those who objected in principle to the idea of SATs and consequently objected to the provision of support to 'make SATs work'. However, these heads also feared for their Y2 teachers if they did *not* offer support. Support, therefore, was laid on to help the teacher, rather than to ensure the success of the SAT exercise.

Quality of support
The quality of support, especially teaching support, was understandably important to the Y2 teachers. In one extreme case the teacher decided to abandon SATs altogether because she felt the support teacher was incapable of handling the rest of the class. Another class teacher felt unhappy about the support teacher's topic work and her way of dealing with it, as well as the support teacher's reference to the class as her own, and her reorganization of it. One school felt their ancillary was not suitable to be in the classroom and would be used only for clerical duties.

The vast majority of teachers (24 out of 30) expressed concern about the activities of the non-SAT children. In observation we witnessed a wide range of activities, including painting, worksheets, looking for frogs outside, making folders, sewing, cutting out pictures, and making peppermint creams. While some teachers had laboriously planned topic work or activities with the supply or support teacher, a few were leaving the curriculum decisions to the covering teacher and expressing concern over their own loss of control. A few also worried about their relationships with children, especially the non-Y2 children in mixed-age classes who had lost day-to-day contact with the teacher. One teacher described deterioration of discipline and lack of care of equipment and felt that his Y1 children were missing contact and attention from him while he conducted SATs over a five-week period.

Only six teachers said that they were happy about the rest of the class. These teachers commented positively on the quality of the support person, feeling that the rest of the class was 'in capable hands', usually while doing a programme of work set by the Y2 teacher and carried out by the support staff.

Lesson to be learnt from the SATs

We asked heads, Y2 teachers and others who administered SATs about the usefulness of the SAT experience. Did SATs offer any insights into teaching and learning? Would teachers change their practice in any way? Were there any implications for curriculum development?

Out of 32 schools, teachers at only one school stated categorically that they had learnt nothing whatsoever: SATs were not revealing anything teachers didn't know already. Fifteen schools *began* by saying that they had learnt nothing to further their understanding but, later, during the interviews, they contradicted this. Sixteen out of the 32 schools felt that administering SATs had been a useful experience, offering room for reflection on curriculum content, individual children's learning and/or the educational process. One head who did an in-house evaluation with her teachers summed up their comments:

> It has certainly taught the staff much about organization, teamwork, forward thinking, planning, assessing, teaching and, last, but not least, enjoyment.

So, virtually all our schools found that they had learnt something from the SAT experience. This is in contrast to the widely reported 'they told me nothing I didn't already know' comments.

Implications for the curriculum

A number of teachers identified gaps in curriculum coverage: they felt that they had learnt that their children were unpractised in certain specific areas. Not surprisingly, these areas were in the core subjects, particularly English and maths. Twenty-one respondents in 19 schools said it was their intention to 'do more' next year – for example, practise capitals and full stops, give children practice in instant recall, and introduce the maths game into class-work. In addition to these concerns about specific curriculum content teachers proposed to broaden the curriculum in different ways, such as doing more practical and investigational work.

Some of these 'gaps' (e.g. instant recall, capitals and full stops) were said to be out of line with the school's beliefs about what was important at this age and would be included only in order to give the children a fair chance in the SATs. Others (e.g. investigational science) were because the teachers had seen these activities as worth while, within the children's abilities and enjoyable. One head felt the staff as a whole would need to 'look in depth at the activities being provided in daily classwork'. One teacher, delighted at her children's response to the writing SAT (when she used the 'being from outer space' idea suggested in the guidance), vowed to 'put real effort into finding a stimulus ... I should be doing this all the time'.

Implications for school development

Heads and members of senior management teams also expressed intentions to relate the SAT experience to whole school issues of organization and curriculum planning.

Seven heads proposed changes in the organization of class groups and two heads had decided to move teachers next year, one of them now certain that 'You don't put your deputy with Y2'. Five schools in the sample felt that 'teams' of two or three teachers (either team-teaching or rotating between classes) worked particularly well and they intended to retain this model of staff deployment. According to one head the mutual support offered in such teams had improved planning, target setting and 'match', and had boosted teachers' confidence in their own personal judgement.

Change in teachers' practice

Teachers' comments seemed to suggest that the administration of SATs had meant a change in normal practice for them. Seventeen respondents representing 15 schools implied they had learnt something which might lead to rethinking, change or development in their pedagogy. Areas for review were concerned with group work, children's independence, task setting, teachers' expectations of individual children and the uptake of miscue analysis.

Seven schools mentioned doing more group work. One school had taped all the children's conversations about the maths game to identify the ways in which individual children contributed. Other schools either saw advantages in group work or discovered that they *could* cope with it. Two heads observed that two Y2 teachers were finding they could *actually* do group work, having previously favoured whole class teaching, though these teachers were in the minority since class teaching is not common at this age.

Two schools mentioned children's independence as learners. One teacher was surprised that she could 'leave them with the maths game

for 10 minutes and when I came back they would be getting on !' Another said she could see she would 'have to get the independent learning going'.
What is clear from this section is that in most schools the SAT experience had given the staff food for thought and many were seriously considering changing their practice in some way. This was only rarely 'teaching to the test', more often it was the result of being offered a wider model of teaching and curriculum.

The implementation of SATs
On our first visit to schools we had specifically noted and asked about the layout of the classrooms, the type of activities planned, use of staff in the class, the teacher's preferred mode of operating with children and how the children were grouped.

SATs as an integrated activity
On our second visit, when we observed the SATs, teachers in 12 class-rooms were operating in a very similar way to that observed on our first visit. As one head put it: 'Teachers are absorbing SATs into normal practice.' These 12 teachers did not make SATs into something special because: the use of space and seating was exactly or very nearly the same as on visit one; the whole class had been planned for by the class teacher, with the SAT group just one of many; the activities were similar to those observed on visit one; non-SAT children did activities like the SATs; four teachers planned SATs into topics; timetabled activities were not necessarily disrupted by SATs; and the staff in classrooms were deployed in the same way as on visit one, i.e. the classroom was managed in the same way. The eight teachers who had ancillary help in the classroom maintained total control of classroom management and curriculum con-tent: they did all the rerouteing, dealt with issues of discipline, answered children's questions, stopped the SAT group when they wanted, or left the SAT group alone and circulated around the others, as they normally did. The ancillaries supervised activities or heard reading as usual. These teachers were observed to be operating in a way closely resembling that of visit one: dealing with whole class issues, sometimes addressing the whole class, going round all groups or working with one group at a time, but occasionally circulating and always controlling the activities of the whole class.
Grouping of children was an area where seven of these teachers did change their arrangements: the teachers with vertically grouped classes,

who usually mixed Y1 or Y3 with Y2, found they were splitting off the Y2 children for the SAT period. One teacher included a Y3 child in a SAT group 'to make up the numbers'. This grouping issue was not a problem for the four teachers with a whole class of Y2 children.

It could be said, then, that in twelve classrooms, SATs were 'built-in' to the usual working pattern. However, there were some abnormal procedures introduced by three teachers in this group who adopted ritual to maintain their concentration on SATs. This consisted of pinning on badges or bows rather like a uniform so that they would not be disturbed. In one school the teacher wore a large, colourful bow; in another school both teacher and SAT group wore badges. The badges and bows symbolized that the teachers were 'off limits', separate, apart, and must not be approached. Once this separation of the SAT group was achieved the three teachers were freed from interruption and could choose their mode of operation, a mode we saw them use in visit one – circulating, supervising work of ancillaries, looking at other children's work and leaving the SAT group alone when necessary. On one occasion, it was difficult to keep the SAT group apart because the non-SAT children forgot the rules. In this case, when a non-SAT child approached the teacher, the teacher merely *pointed* to her badge; no words were exchanged and the child moved off to sort out her problem herself.

SATs as a bolt-on activity

In the other 20 schools the way in which SATs were managed led to a certain 'artificiality' in daily classroom routine. One head called it: 'A false situation, totally controlled and unreal in the classroom'.

Twelve of these classrooms had been reorganized to provide a special SAT area – usually two tables and five chairs (one for each child and the teacher) – in a corner or other part of the classroom that was somehow separate. The other children usually seemed to know that this area was meant only for SAT activities.

Teachers and heads in these 20 schools gave three reasons for this sense of artificiality:

- planning two separate timetables/different activities;
- intensive concentration on certain groups; and
- sharing children and giving away responsibility.

One teacher with a mixed-age class thought she would be able to work SATs into her usual 'class structure', but could not. Instead, she planned in an artificial way during the SATs period: one timetable for Y2 and another for Y3. Normally, she would plan for the class as a whole, regardless of year group.

One head mentioned how the teachers were extra tired because of the 'intensive concentration' on small numbers of children. Withdrawing children from the classroom, as a strategy for implementation, may have exacerbated this. Seventeen schools in this group of 20 withdrew children: five for reading only; eight for other SATs; and four for both reading and other SATs. The three other teachers did not leave the classroom but neither did they leave the SAT group during the assessment. The fact that they did not leave the SAT group could have led to a feeling of intensive concentration and also to an unfamiliar feeling of being 'unavailable' to non-SAT children, which was mentioned by two of these teachers.

To support SATs in these schools, other adults moved in, or were moved into classrooms, as described in a previous section. In ten schools teachers seemed willingly to accept the help of others and made no reference to this extra help being artificial to classroom processes. However, the other ten teachers made special mention of the support adding to the artificiality that SATs lent to daily routine. From comments made in their interviews, and from our observation, it was noted that these ten teachers accommodated help but were ambivalent about it.

For teachers in these 20 schools, then, SATs involved all or most of the following changes: newly created classroom layouts/withdrawal groups; planning different activities for year groups; sharing teaching and giving away responsibility; and operating in a different way (e.g. being unavailable to some children). What emerges however is that, regardless of whether the SATs were integrated into the normal teaching activity or bolted-on to it, considerable extra effort and organization were involved for the teacher.

Emerging themes
A number of analytic themes emerged from our data.

Protecting children
A major theme is that of protecting children. All of our 32 schools seemed to take the view that SATs should not be presented to children as testing, that it was in the best interest of the children not to know they were being tested. The dilemma then was how to encourage best performance without making testing an issue. There were differing views as to how

much awareness children actually had of SATs, but all schools seemed to believe that 'doing the right thing' meant protecting children from the (perceived) pressures of testing (and possible failure).

Several schools commented that they were trying to 'keep things as normal as possible' and some teachers chose to introduce SATs as normal activities, or as a game. SATs were kept low-key in most schools and in half the schools steps were taken to disguise SATs either as normal activity, or as something different but fun. Schools referred to SATs by various names: 'special work', 'group work', 'experiments', 'games', etc. in an attempt to 'minimize the whole experience'. Disguising SATs sometimes extended to avoiding 'exiting' children from the task because the teacher did not want to 'single anyone out'; this was particularly true of the reading SAT, in which children were quite often allowed to continue reading the book, or have it read to them, after it was clear that they were not achieving at a particular level.

Schools adopted a number of practices in their attempts to protect SAT children from disruptions from non-SAT children. These included: using screens to partition off the SATs area from the rest of the class; withdrawing children into 'cozy quiet rooms' for SATs to give them 'the best possible chance'; and keeping the SAT children in the class-room with their teacher while the rest of the class was taken out by someone else. In one class the teacher saw herself as an obstacle: 'I've noticed before that they tend not to talk together when I'm there, so I left them to get on with it for a little while.'

Encouraging best performance

Some teachers were concerned that aspects of the SATs would be unfamiliar to children and might make them perform less well so they gave them what can only be described as practice, for example with worksheets.

Some teachers chose groupings carefully in order to give certain children a better chance. This involved: 'avoiding pairs that get up to mischief'; putting 'an insensitive child, who would say "you're not doing it right" with a very confident child who wouldn't mind such comments'; keeping the same group together throughout all the SATs so that it would be 'less unsettling' for them all; and putting the bilingual children together. Sometimes teachers had to ensure that quiet children spoke up. One teacher was observed repeatedly trying to stop a bossy child from taking over her weaker, quieter partner.

Teachers protected SATs children from failure by giving extra chances in various ways. Some teachers administered SATs to a child individually, usually because the child was quiet and would not have performed well within a group, or was too upset after trying to work in a group. Teachers also found reasons for retesting children to give them another chance to succeed because the teacher felt they could do it. In one school three classes of Y2 children were retested on a maths SAT after they had all done less well than expected. The three teachers met to 'standardize' together and agreed to give 'extra goes'. Several teachers reported situations where they had 'not stuck to the letter of the law' in administering SATs. Hints and nudges were observed in cases where teachers were anxious for children to achieve.

Reassurance
We observed many instances where teachers reassured children either about the tasks in general or about specific aspects of a task in which the child was having difficulty. Some teachers prefaced the SAT task, as in the case of choosing reading books, with 'It doesn't matter if it looks too hard and you can't read it, just try it if you like it'. (This was also an attempt to disguise the reading SAT as a test.) Another teacher, telling her children about a maths task, said: 'We haven't done these sort before at all so it's only for fun – funny sort of fun, but there you are, don't worry about it.'

Some teachers were observed reassuring children about their unusual behaviour during the SAT, especially in respect of recording in the SEAC record book. Some teachers explained to children that they would be ticking off words as the child read. Another said: 'I've written things down, just in case I forget.' Other teachers chose not to use the SEAC book at all and devised other means of recording so that the children would not see the unfamiliar book.

Some teachers assured children throughout the SAT that 'it doesn't matter if you get it wrong' and 'the spelling doesn't matter'. Others offered reassurance throughout, such as: 'Nearly, nearly got it right.'; 'Don't worry about it.'; 'Is it too hard?'; 'You're allowed to give up.' There were also reports, though no observations, of children being 'talked through' a SAT after becoming upset.

Protecting non-SAT children
The majority of our teachers expressed concern about non-SAT children. This concern revolved around the 'lack of meaningful activities', the

'loss of teaching time' and the lack of contact between teachers and non-SAT children over the SATs period which one head referred to as producing 'withdrawal symptoms'.

Some of this concern was expressed as guilt: 'I have tremendous guilt so they are going outside more than usual to give them something fun and interesting to do.' One teacher explained to her 'neglected' children that this part of the term would be 'like this' (i.e. disrupted) but she clearly felt guilt over the activities of her non-SAT children. Another teacher promised her Y1 children, 'In three weeks we can do something very interesting' because she knew they were keen to design and make things, which she could not supervise over the SATs period in her vertically grouped class.

Teachers felt it was 'important not to make non-SAT children feel excluded' and that they should have a 'definite activity' while SATs were going on. Some teachers liked to 'settle everybody' before they began SATs, introducing the class-work as usual. Maintaining routine also meant that non-SATs children should have access to their teacher, so badges and bows and other means of keeping them away from SATs were thought to be wrong by some teachers: 'After all, we're here to help the children, not to turn around and say "don't disturb me now".' One teacher dealt with the children's interest in wobbly teeth on the spot as a way of maintaining the usual routine of the classroom.

Some teachers claimed that their non-SAT children 'suffered' over the SATs period, giving various activities that had been affected because of reorganization in the school or classroom. PE, music, arts and crafts, CDT, country dancing and extra curricular activities were some of the things which were said to be 'getting lost' during SATs. Of more concern was the lack of time to hear children read, which several schools reported. Others mentioned lack of time to prepare children for the junior school and, in the case of Catholic schools, to prepare children for their first communion.

A few teachers felt that they had to stop SATs when non-SAT children became too badly affected. One teacher stopped a SAT when he saw classroom activities of non-SAT children coming to an end and an auxiliary not knowing what to do next. Another teacher temporarily abandoned SATs because things were not going well for the non-SAT children and the support teacher: the Y2 teacher wanted to stop SATs and 'take charge of the class, settle them down and get back to a working routine'. She was prepared to do this despite the head's insistence that she carry on with SATs. ('No one is going to put me in prison if I don't finish.')

Guilt and anxiety

Guilt was often mentioned by our teachers in relation to the experiences of both the SAT and non-SAT children. There was also guilt in relation to devolving responsibility to support teachers, and losing contact with non-SAT children, particularly younger and/or newer children. Some of this anxiety was rooted in their concern for how children were experiencing the presence and role of the other adults. Teachers commented on children's 'upset' or 'confusion' over the change in routine, one reporting that children were confused because the head was 'babysitting' and an ancillary was 'occupying the class'. Another teacher imagined how a child must feel who was removed from the classroom to be 'alone in a room with three adults and a tape recorder'. As she remarked: 'You can see it's not a normal thing.'

Raised professionalism

In the interviews, raised professionalism of Y2 teachers was reported in one-third of the schools, either by heads or the teachers themselves. Examples included leading their Y2 colleagues and doing assessment training with the junior teachers.

In the observations, groups of teachers in eight schools altogether were seen by us to have become more interested and more active in diagnostic assessment. Indicators of this interest included detailed discussion of individual children, considerable in-house moderation, reflection on their own practice, note-taking throughout the SATs and the consideration and discussion of questions to ask the children.

In the interviews it also became clear that six schools were analysing the SAT experience, asking further questions and intended to develop practice in some way. We refer to these as analytic schools and we will be following their development over the next year. Heads and teachers in these schools made both general and specific comments about what they had learnt about the teaching/learning dynamic, for example how their teachers had, in general, improved their powers of observation and their focus on individual needs.

This sort of professional development was clearly easier to engender in a school where more than one teacher was involved in the SATs. One of the most exciting schools to visit was a first school where all the teachers were involved: the level of participation, discussion and raised awareness was quite marked. At the other extreme was a young probationary teacher, with a whole class of Y2 children, who was the only person in her school doing SATs. Even so, she was observed to be

administering SATs in a highly proficient, sensitive, relaxed and supportive manner. She was able to do this despite having no colleague involved
in the same exercise.

Conclusions

A picture has emerged of considerable changes made to support the
administration of SATs. In some schools this had a knock-on effect on
other staff and where disruption was widespread it contributed to stress
within the school. Collegial support for Y2 teachers was the rule rather
than the exception. High levels of support were to protect Y2 teachers
rather than ensure the SATs were done particularly well or quickly; less
support was needed in schools with vertical grouping and/or team
teaching. In half the schools the heads were actively involved in the SATs
or support activities and welcomed the opportunity to spend time with
the children. There were lessons to be learnt in relation to curriculum
coverage, styles of teaching and learning and classroom management,
but little in relation to assessment *per se* beyond finding close observation rewarding ('if only we had the time ...'). There was also little
acceptance by the teachers themselves that the detailed assessment task
had shown anything about individual children which their own informal
assessment had not.

Assessment in relation to the SATs was more likely to be a bolt-on
than an integrated activity. Early studies of TA have given conflicting
pictures in relation to teachers' practice in this area: Harlen and Qualter
(1991) found that teachers did not recognize their informal judgements
as 'assessment' for TA; they felt they needed to add a special task as a
formal check. Broadfoot, *et al.* (1991) on the other hand report that there
is some evidence that teachers are becoming more confident and skilled
in assessment, and more able to be flexible in their approach, integrating
teaching and assessment. This is to be welcomed since, as Harlen and
Qualter point out, making judgements based on special tasks takes away
one of the values of TA; that, since information comes from a range of
contexts rather than one, its reliability is greater. The situation with
regard to SATs is rather different: it was almost inevitable that they be
seen as an added or bolt-on activity. Given the lack of choice, the lack
of cross-curricular tasks and the difficulty of working the activities into
a topic (all of which were promised in the TGAT report), not to mention
the size of the task for teachers with high numbers of children to assess,
it is almost surprising that *any* schools managed to integrate the SATs
into their regular classroom activities. It is also worth asking how likely

it is that any mandated, high-stakes assessment will become absorbed rather than treated as 'special' or extra.

In schools which we describe as analytic, where teachers discussed criteria and standards of performance, it is likely that assessments were more standardized and comparable across classes than in other schools. With regard to criterion-referenced assessment, it was clear that the statements were not always clear enough for teachers to make unambiguous judgements about performance. It is also clear, however, that in some schools this very fact contributed to discussion and within-school moderation. Teachers' expertise in relation to criterion-referenced assessment is still embryonic: there was evidence that they were reacting to the outcome level in relation to some form of ranking and/or norming, (e.g. 'that's not a level 3 child').

It was common for teachers to try to get the best performance out of children: by reassuring them, helping them, offering preparation and support, and sometimes offering a second chance. This is one of the criteria for educational assessment (Wood, 1986) and definitely runs counter to the notion of assessment as examination, or hurdle. This may have been due not necessarily to any particular view of assessment, but to the teachers' view of what is appropriate for children of this age. Teachers were concerned about failure and 'labelling' for such young children and there was some tension between offering children the chance to try the next level up or to keep going at a lower level task, thereby preventing failure.

A number of factors point to the teachers' professionalism: the eagerness to support colleagues; the considerable efforts to 'make it work'; the concern over the non-SAT children; that stress and irritability were rarely seen with the children (i.e. during the SAT) or in relation to non-SAT children, but came out in other ways or in other parts of the teachers' lives; the concern to protect children etc. In addition, the anxiety over the quality of support cover and the children's experience highlights the very close relationship between teacher and child at this age. Support was a massive and by no means straightforward issue: where class teachers kept control of the support teacher by setting the work and keeping tabs on the class, they generally felt less guilty and anxious about the effect of this arrangement on the children. This, of course, meant more work for the teachers.

Stress was widespread but the level differed from school to school. There is no doubt that stress and tiredness were real; what is not clear is how much of this was due to the size and scale of the innovation or to its high profile, and how much was due to it being assessment *per se* with all that this means for the teacher/child relationship and anxiety over performance. The children, however, were generally unaware of the purpose and importance of the tasks they were engaged in. This was because teachers were at great pains to ensure that they were protected from what was going on. Very few children were seen to be upset by the activities; some were bored but many enjoyed them.

Ironically, despite the problems with the content of this particular innovation, its size, scope and compulsory nature have led to what can only be described as increased collegiality. As Fullan (1991) points out, Goodlad concluded that teachers traditionally work under conditions of autonomous isolation rather than rich professional dialogue. Fullan's own work shows that the degree of change undertaken by teachers is strongly related to the extent to which teachers interact with each other and those providing help. Within the school, collegiality among teachers, as measured by the frequency of communication, mutual support and help, etc. was a strong indicator of implementation success. What we observed in a number of schools was clearly the development of what Hargreaves and Dawe (1989) call a collaborative culture, rather than contrived collegiality which may be short-lived. This is one of the ideal conditions for real innovation to take place. We have the possibility of real innovation and professional development here despite the problems with the SATs. What we can hope for is that some expertise in relation to assessment will survive this, in many cases traumatic, experience. More significantly at this stage we hope that increased levels of collegiality will be retained enabling those schools to deal with the coming challenges in a positive and professional way.

What about the nature of the assessment programme itself? What can we learn that is of benefit to those in the USA urging the use of 'authentic' or performance-based assessment? Standardized testing has been criticized for being based on faulty learning-theory assumptions (Resnick and Resnick, 1991), viz. decomposability and decontextualization. The first of these relates to the belief that complex behaviours can be broken down into a collection of independent pieces of knowledge, and that the ability to perform complex tasks can be assessed through a sample of the component pieces. However, recent cognitive research has shown that complex skills and competencies rely not just on the number of components they involve but also on interactions among them and heuristics for calling upon them. Thus testing isolated components in standardized tests, which encourages the teaching of isolated components, is unlikely to lead to students learning to do, for example, real problem solving or interpretive thinking. The second faulty assumption is decontextualization. Knowledge and skill cannot be detached from their contexts of practice and use. As much recent work on assessment has shown we cannot validly assess a skill in a context which is very different from the context in which it is practised or used.

As Shepard (1991) points out, in a system which is dominated by standardized tests, these assumptions shape the daily mode of instruction, leading to repeated drill on isolated skills. Furthermore, Shepard argues that emphasis on raising test scores reinforces other behaviourist principles held in schools, like the idea that thinking and reasoning should be postponed until after basic skills have been mastered. So, poor test performers get more drill while only high scorers are provided with instruction aimed at teaching comprehension and problem solving. The argument in the US currently is that bringing in authentic assessments will change the focus of teachers' activities in teaching to the test: 'Authentic assessment supports good teaching by not requiring teachers to redirect attention away from important concepts, in-depth projects, and the like.'

What we can say is that the the 1991 KS1 SATs were designed on an authentic assessment model. Despite anxiety over the quality of the worksheets, they matched the active process-based tasks which children do in good infant classroom practice much more closely than do traditional standardized tests. As our data shows, these assessment tasks not only gave our teachers direct ideas for areas of the curriculum which they had not covered, but also, for some, pointers towards a wider view of teaching and learning. This is the opposite of the traditional concept of teaching to the test – which is typically viewed as narrowing and negative – in that it widened teachers' practice rather than narrowed it. Thus, from this experience we can say that the introduction of high-stakes, authentic assessment can broaden teachers' practice in much the same way as the introduction of high-stakes minimum competency or traditional standardized tests tends to narrow teachers' practice.

On this basis we can hypothesize that the move away from using process-based tasks and any attempt to return to narrow paper and pencil tests of the traditional, limited, standardized type will effect a narrowing of teaching again. The prospect is daunting, and emphasizes the waste of time, energy and money that has resulted from this exercise. As Fullan has it (Fullan, 1991, p. 345): 'The shame of educational change is the squandering of good intentions and the waste of resources in light of personal and societal needs of great human consequence.'

References

Baker, E. and Stites, R. (1991) 'Trends in Testing in the USA.' *Politics of Education Association Yearbook, 1990.* Taylor & Francis.

Broadfoot, P., Abbott, D., Croll, P., Osborn, M., Pollard, A. and Towler, L. (1991) 'Implementing National Assessment: issues for primary teachers.' *Cambridge Journal of Education*, Vol. 21, No. 2.

Fullan, M. (1991) *The New Meaning of Educational Change.* Cassell Educational Ltd.

Hargreaves, A. and Dawe, R. (1989) *Coaching as Unreflective Practice: contrived collegiality or collaborative culture?* Paper presented at AERA meeting.

Harlen, W. and Qualter, A. (1991) 'Issues in SAT Development and the Practice of Teacher Assessment.' *Cambridge Journal of Education*, Vol. 21, No. 2.

Resnick, L. and Resnick, D. (1991) 'Assessing the Thinking Curriculum: new tools for educational reform.' In: Gifford, B. and O'Connor, M. (eds) *Future Assessments: changing views of aptitude, achievement and instruction.* Kluwer Academic Publishers.

Shepard, L. (1991) 'Interview on Assessment Issues with Lorrie Shepard.' *Educational Researcher*, Vol. 20, No. 2, March 1991.

Wood, R. (1986) 'The Agenda for Educational Measurement.' In: Nuttall, D. L. (ed.) *Assessing Educational Achievement.* Lewes: Falmer Press.

Chapter Seven
The Power of the Key Stage Cops – Recording and Reporting Requirements: Their Effect on Formative Assessment Practice

Pat Tunstall

Introduction

Some 6-year-olds were making a model house. The teacher wanted to assess AT6 in Science, Level 2, 'be able to recognize important similarities and differences, including hardness, flexibility and transparency, in the characteristics of materials' and AT10 in Maths, Level 2, 'recognize squares...rectangular boxes...cylinders...and describe them'. The teacher therefore put together an assortment of various materials including some boxes.

What the children said and did	*What the teacher thought*
Jason said the roof should be 'like a triangle'.	Does this mean Jason recognizes triangles?
Thu-Hein and Amya decided to put carpet in their house. Amya got a ruler to measure it but was not sure which way round to use it. Thu-Hein read 26 as 62.	Amya knows what rulers are for but cannot interpret them. Thu-Hein needs some work on place value.
Daraksheim said you didn't need a slopey roof - the classroom has a flat roof. Kirsty said they had a flat roof and it leaked	Good comments but I'd need to see this in other contexts before I could say they were at level 3.
Thu-Hein said they needed something see-through for the windows and Amya suggested sweet-papers.	Does this mean that they understand transparency?

The example of practice described above is drawn from *Teacher Assessment: Making it Work in the Primary School* (Association for Science Education, 1990). The teacher is shown gathering information about children's understanding in relation to Statements of Attainment (SoAs), making qualitative judgements and deciding what to do next in order to take learning forward. The example represents an approach to formative assessment practice within the National Curriculum which has been encouraged in schools across the country. In National Curriculum assessment procedures, reporting data have their basis in records relating to observations of this kind.

TGAT judged that an assessment system designed for formative purposes could equally meet the identified summative and evaluative needs of national assessment at ages before 16. In implementing that judgement, one basic assessment procedure, that of aggregation of scores within the National Curriculum levels, was accepted for National Curriculum assessment. Aggregation entails SoAs being combined into profile component levels and profile component levels into overall subject levels. The Orders for Key Stage 1, which set out the rules for aggregation in the only Key Stage as yet fully operational, put the TGAT hypothesis into statutory effect; the records of teacher assessment (TA), combined with the results of the Standard Assessment Tasks (SATs), are turned into data by which an individual's performance can be reported to parents, and teacher and school effectiveness can be measured.

Critics have contended that TGAT was attempting to 'square the circle' (Brighouse and Moon, 1990, p. 7), to 'reconcile the irreconcilable' (Nuttall, 1989), in combining formative and summative purposes. It is apparent that requirements in the area of recording and reporting have an impact on the status of formative assessment. Early but important examples of the way reporting requirements affected any balance of purpose in National Curriculum Assessment were the decisions about reporting by profile components (PCs). TGAT had recommended that a small number of PCs should be created in each subject area for reporting purposes; at the same time, however, it was TGAT's view that PCs should have a formative role being of a type 'to which pupils can respond and which clearly indicate what has been and what remains to be achieved'. In the form accepted by the Secretary of State, PCs were reduced, for example, in science to two. As Tom Christie indicated (1990, p. 197), the second PC, 'Knowledge and understanding of science, communication and the applications and implications of science', has '15 different Attainment Targets rolled into one' making any report in terms of science PC2 'essentially uninterpretable'. PC information in science has had little relevance in terms of useful information to be passed on to secondary schools or curriculum planning at any stage. The need for simple summative reporting data took priority even though it became meaningless for feedback purposes. Such a position will be history with the introduction in August 1992 of the new Orders for science and maths in which the number of Attainment Targets (ATs) are reduced and PCs are scrapped. Nonetheless, it is important to examine current recording and reporting requirements as a whole for the ways in which they continue to affect the balance between the formative, summative and evaluative purposes of the National Curriculum. This chapter sets out the requirements and demonstrates the resulting tensions and shifts in emphasis.

RECORDING

Statutory requirements
The requirements for recording are laid down under two sections of the Education Reform Act. The requirements are: the Regulations for School Records 1989 and the Assessment Orders for Key Stage 1.

• *The Regulations (School Records) 1989 made under Section 218 (1) (f) of the Education Reform Act*
These Regulations cover two areas: the keeping of records and access to records. Governing bodies are required, as from 1 September 1989, to keep records on every registered pupil at the school. This 'curricular record', which is to be updated once a year for each pupil, must include material on the pupil's academic achievements, other skills and abilities and progress in school. Governing bodies are also required, as from 1 September 1990 to allow the parent of a registered pupil aged under 18, or a registered pupil if aged 16 or over, access to that pupil's record. The Regulations also deal with the transfer of a pupil's records to other educational establishments.

Circular 17/89 accompanies the Regulations. This Circular makes it clear that the 'Regulations do not prescribe how the records should be kept or lay down any detailed requirements as to their contents'. Schools and LEAs are advised that they should aim to keep their recording systems simple but that two distinct purposes must be served: the need to be able to present to other teachers and the parents concerned basic data on how any given pupil is progressing within any given AT; and the need for teachers to be able to support their assessments of pupils' levels of attainment, in particular at the end of Key Stages.

The Circular also goes on to say that as statutory assessments are concerned with levels of pupils' knowledge, skills and understanding, there is no statutory need for teachers to collect and retain large volumes of evidence throughout the Key Stage.

The Regulations, with the guidance offered by the accompanying Circular, provide the existing basis within the Education Reform Act for the records of teachers' ongoing, formative assessments.

• *The Orders for Key Stage 1 (the Education (National Curriculum) Assessment Arrangements for English, Mathematics and Science Order 1990), updated in July 1991, made under Section 4*
These Orders generated recording requirements for the end of Key Stage 1. The Orders require: a record of the results of TA to be made in the form of a level of attainment achieved by the pupil in relation to every AT; a record of the results of the SAT assessment in the form of a statement of each level of attainment achieved by each pupil in relation to each relevant AT; a record of a statement consisting of each pupil's overall level of attainment in each core subject and each AT and PC in each subject, derived through a given process of aggregation.

The Orders for Key Stage 1 do not include requirements about teacher records throughout the Key Stage but, as the accompanying Circular 9/90 makes clear, there are implications. In discussing TA, the Circular states that it is not a requirement of the Order that teachers should assess each pupil 'fully and afresh against every AT at the end of the Key Stage', but must maintain a record of each pupil's attainments.

Summary of focus of the statutory requirements
The focus of the requirements can be summed up in this way:

- the Regulations for School Records require schools to keep ongoing records but neither they nor the accompanying Circular prescribe content in any detail;
- the Orders for Key Stage 1 relate only to the summative reporting end of Key Stage, with the accompanying Circular containing minimal discussion of records throughout the Key Stage.

Policy implementation

Implementation of the requirements for recording is mainly being undertaken through the provision of: central advice by SEAC and the DES; INSET and support by LEAs.

Advice on recording
• *SEAC: A Guide to Teacher Assessment Packs A, B and C.*
If TA is indeed to be formative assessment, backed up by recording procedures which support teachers in making valid and fair judgements of children's progress, it might have been expected that non-statutory guidance would have been produced. There seems to be little doubt that SEAC's Packs A, B and C were meant to perform this function. The Packs demonstrate a formidable logic being applied to formative assessment. In Packs A, B and C, SoAs are central to the whole practice of daily assessment within the classroom and are to be applied in a unified approach across the curriculum. Pack C's chapter on recording provides some examples of approaches to recording SoAs along with a section which discusses the evaluation of record-keeping procedures.

The general response to the SEAC Packs was reported by HMI in their booklet, *Assessment, Recording and Reporting* (DES, 1991). 'The materials were not well received in some schools and generated anxiety among teachers because they were considered to be largely irrelevant to the task being faced at that time.' The chapter on recording, with its emphasis on SoAs, may have generated such anxiety.

• *SEAC: School Assessment Folder 1990/91*
This folder gave advice on the completion of TA and included two documents: Document A for summarizing TA and SAT results in order to reach the overall levels; and Document B which could be used by teachers to record SoAs achieved throughout the Key Stage. The Assessment Folder suggests rules for aggregating TA and, in a very different tenor from SEAC's Pack C, provides some fairly gentle prompting about ongoing teacher records:

> One method of completing Document A will be for you to reflect on your existing general records and what you remember of each child's work over the previous two years. Some teachers in the pilot found this method difficult however...
>   Another method is for you to maintain systematic records of achieved statements of attainment throughout the Key Stage but particularly in Year 2...Some teachers used a combination of the two methods.

The advice states that Document B is not a requirement; it is clear, however, that in SEAC's view it is advisable to keep ongoing records of SoAs.

• *SEAC: Teacher Assessment at Key Stage 3*
This leaflet, published in 1991, states:

> Recording attainment should take place throughout the Key Stage. There is no nationally prescribed way of keeping these records. The procedures for continuous TA and the format of records of attainment are matters for local professional judgement and are best decided within schools.

The leaflet also has some advice about collecting evidence, stating that: 'It is not necessary to attempt to collect evidence of everything a pupil attains, but rather to be able to point to key examples of achievement that support particular judgements.'

LEA responsibilities in policy implementation

LEA funding for National Curriculum Assessment Implementation Plans depends on criteria which include responsibility for enabling schools to 'maintain simple and manageable record-keeping systems that will enable assessment data to be used formatively, that is, in deciding the next steps in learning for each pupil' and 'ensure that records are adequate for the completion of the TA for each pupil...as well as being sufficient to inform the annual report to parents in that year and other years of the Key Stage' (SEAC, 1990a). Training for teachers is also a prerequisite in the LEA Implementation Plans. As a result, LEAs have engaged in a great deal of trialling and experimentation in record keeping. The National Curriculum Council's *Report on Monitoring the Implementation of the National Curriculum Core Subjects 1989–90* (NCC, 1991) commented on the fact that the London boroughs had a higher proportion of recommended systems for core subjects at Key Stage 1 than the rest of the country; this was attributed to the use of the Primary Language Record which has been adapted for the core subjects as a Primary Learning Record. In the country as a whole, however, it was reported that 'several LEAs were postponing firm decisions on record keeping until national policy on assessment and reporting had been clarified'.

Summary of focus of advice on recording

Clear statements about the use of assessment as a support to learning are present in SEAC documents. Along with that, central advice is clearly linking formative assessment with the need to keep records of attainment levels. Teachers are being told in varying degrees of firmness that they should keep records of SoAs throughout a Key Stage and evidence by way of samples of work even though the basis for such advice is not fully articulated by Regulations, Circulars or Orders. Apart from SEAC's Packs A, B and C, there is little guidance available at central level for teachers on how records should be kept. Teachers have looked to their LEAs for support or devised their own school approaches.

Policy in practice

Confusion
In view of the advice provided, it is interesting that both research findings and a report from HMI indicate that teachers have been thoroughly confused by the requirements.

Research carried out by the University of Warwick, commissioned by the Assistant Masters and Mistresses Association (University of Warwick, 1991), reports widespread confusion about record keeping. The report, *Workloads, Achievement and Stress*, states that this confusion was generating fear and anxiety in schools with the result that Year 2 teachers were spending over eight to nine hours per week on marking and recording. In the writers' view, teachers perceived 'a policy vacuum or, at best, policy confusion' in terms of recording. 'We believe that in spring 1991, their situation was akin to what one French sociologist called "anomie" – a state in which clear expectations for behaviour were absent.' Such a state was reported to be driving teachers and their headteachers to devise a vast range of approaches to record keeping for fear that 'the Key Stage Cops' would appear from around some corner.

This state of confusion is also described in the interim report of the NFER/BGC research consortium, entitled *Teacher Assessment at Key Stage 3* (SEAC, 1991a). The report states that there was major uncertainty and confusion in areas of record keeping. Teachers frequently said that national guidelines or a standardized approach to record keeping were needed. Uncertainty about level of detail and even purpose was reported.

Equally, HMI in their booklet *Assessment, Recording and Reporting* (DES, 1991), which reports on the first year of the implementation of the curricular requirements of the Education Reform Act, describe the variations in practice observed in schools and state that many teachers need to be 'clearer about the purposes of assessment, recording and reporting'.

Researchers and HMI set down some of the key issues which were causing confusion for teachers. It is apparent that the kind of recording policy decisions teachers are having to make for themselves relate to fundamental aspects of National Curriculum assessment which the Regulations for School Records, the Assessment Orders for Key Stage 1 and the supporting advice all fail to address adequately. These issues include: the level of detail at which the assessment is made and kept; the timing of assessment and whether it is up to date at the end of the Key Stage; recording formats; time and materials management (e.g. keeping samples of work); and the suitability of SoAs as assessment criteria.

Teachers' professional judgement

Reference to teachers' professional judgements is a feature of much of the advice relating to recording requirements. If professional judgements are to be made with a due sense of their value and validity, there must be an existing framework which at least provides a coherent rationale. Such a framework is lacking in terms of teacher records throughout the Key Stage. The work on the new ATs continues to reflect a piecemeal approach without overall regard for conceptual clarity.

Overall trends in recording

In discussing the reasons for confusion in terms of recording, both the writers of the research reports and HMI describe general trends which were apparent in their discussions with teachers. All concur in their message about what is happening to formative practice. HMI state that: 'The purposes of assessment, in particular the value and use of assessment in supporting learning, were not made explicit in over three-quarters of assessment, recording and reporting policies. Further discussion leading to a policy statement would counterbalance the present preoccupation with the summative aspects of assessment.' The University of Warwick report refers to an 'end of Key Stage drift in assessment and recording because the statutory requirements are largely concerned with this period' and goes on to state:

> our interviews with teachers lead us to believe that the formative purpose had largely been excluded from their thinking about assessment which was dominated by concerns to achieve a summative purpose, that is, to allocate pupils to levels so as to provide a basis for comparison between pupils, classes and schools.

REPORTING

The statutory requirements

The requirements for reporting are introduced mainly under Section 22 of the Education Reform Act. This section empowers the Secretary of State to make Regulations concerning the provision of information either generally or to prescribed persons about the curriculum for maintained schools, the educational provision made by schools and the educational achievements of their pupils. Section 22 thus relates to reporting at both school and individual level.

At the time of writing, there are two sets of Regulations relating to reporting assessment: the Individual Pupils' Achievements (Information) Regulations 1990; and the Education (Information on School Examination Results) (England) Regulations 1991. Further Regulations about reporting school assessment results are imminent as a result of the introduction of the Education (Schools) Bill.

• *The Individual Pupils' Achievements (Information) Regulations 1990*
These Regulations for reporting came into force progressively from August 1990. The Regulations are accompanied by Circular 8/90 and apply to all maintained and grant maintained schools in England and Wales. They impose a duty on headteachers to provide a written report each year to parents of all pupils from Years 1 to 13. Parents must receive the reports by 31 July except in Years 11, 12 and 13 when the final date is extended to 30 September.

Reports must now specify at the end of the Key Stage the individual pupil's level of achievement on the 1 to 10 scale by PC and subject for any foundation subject where Orders apply. Details of GCSE results or any other qualifications or certificates have to be included. The requirement to report starts from the year in which pupils are first liable to follow ATs and Programmes of Study. Teachers are required to report progress in every National Curriculum subject even if the Orders for the subject are not in place. The Regulations additionally require 'brief particulars' of the pupil's achievements in any other subjects or activities. Reports must also make clear where pupils have been exempted from any ATs. As mentioned in the section on recording above, these Regulations give parents the right of access on demand to information on the levels of achievement in terms of ATs 'in respect of which the pupil has been assessed in accordance with the statutory arrangements'.

The Circular 8/90 'Records of Achievement' which accompanies the Regulations is important. This Circular attempts to provide a broader vision of reporting than that conveyed by the Regulations: the Regulations should be seen as 'setting a floor' on what must be done in terms of reporting to parents but they do not 'impose a ceiling'.

The Circular recognizes the importance of recording achievement from the pupils' perspective, not solely therefore for the purposes of providing information to parents, and goes on to endorse the formative processes of recording achievement. It also provides important amplification of the Regulations. It is pointed out, for example, that while the Regulations do not require schools to accompany a report of statutory assessment scores with any narrative commentary, it is expected that most schools will do so. The Circular comments that although parents have the right of access on demand to AT level information, it will be for schools to decide the extent to which their reports on statutory assessments should be amplified routinely by AT data. Notice of the intention to devise an agreed common format for reporting is also contained within the Circular.

The Circular commends the principles of recording achievement which are included with the Circular as Annex B. It is important to note in the Annex that the Secretary of State endorses the principle that 'the final summary document should be the property of the school leaver who should have control over its distribution and use'. This point will be picked up later.

• *The Education (Information on School Examination Results) (England) Regulations 1991*

These Regulations and Circular 9/91 which accompanies them relate to the wider aspect of reporting. Schools are required to publish their results in GCSE, A/AS level and other public examinations to parents and the community in a 'common and consistent form'. In 1981, a general requirement to publish GCSE and A/AS levels had been imposed on schools; these Regulations extend that requirement, by specifying in greater detail the form in which the results are to be published. GCSE and A/AS results for each school are to be summarized in a consistent format each year so that comparisons can be made with those 'for the school, the LEA and England in the preceding year'. These Regulations are a foretaste of the promised requirements for reporting National Curriculum results at other Key Stages signalled by the Schools Bill.

Summary of Regulations
In introducing the Regulations on reporting Individual Pupils' Achievements, the DES adopted a minimalistic approach in order to limit the demands made on teachers. Circular 8/90, however, gave a firm indication that Records of Achievement processes and products were being reinstated, a year after Angela Rumbold was believed to be sounding their death-knell. The right of parents to know about their children's progress in school was linked by the DES with formative approaches to assessment and recording.

The Regulations in Information on School Examination Results extend the information to be made available to parents, with the purpose of enabling comparisons to be made between the success of schools on the basis of 'raw scores'. The use of the word 'client' is indicative of the purpose of the requirements which will enable market forces to be applied to schools on the basis of their assessment results. Regulations on reporting data for National Curriculum assessments are expected to be of a similar kind. The Parents' Charter, by its endorsement of the use of 'league tables', indicated the Government's intention of introducing requirements for reporting Key Stage results that will enable comparisons to be made. Further Regulations under Section 22 will result from the Schools Bill.

Policy implementation
In implementing the policy on reporting, the DES has been involved in a number of initiatives.

Formats
The DES has been involved in the central design and even distribution of formats where reporting purposes are concerned. The exercise of teachers' professional judgement does not appear to be required at the summative end of assessment procedures.

The Regulations on Reporting and the Circular on Records of Achievement were followed up with formats in three ways:

(1)   the publication of a standard reporting format for reporting to parents with accompanying explanatory leaflets;

(2)   the launch of the National Record of Achievement (NRA) in a collaborative enterprise between the DES and the Employment Department; and

(3) the design of prototype formats for the publication of School Examination results.

Policy in practice

The HMI's *Assessment, Recording and Reporting* booklet reflects on practice in reporting to parents and Records of Achievement. In referring to Records of Achievement explicitly, HMI are keen to emphasize the need for schools to integrate their Record of Achievement practice with both the recording and reporting of attainment. In commenting on primary school reports, HMI state that the main issue was 'how much information about a child's achievement should be given to parents so that reports remained understandable'. Writing about secondary school reports, HMI comment 'Much more development work needs to be done both centrally and locally to make reports clear to parents'. Both of these comments provide useful statements to examine the way in which the DES itself is providing advice about these areas.

In terms of the wider aspects of reporting examination results, August and September 1991 saw the first league tables of schools with the 'best' results drawn up by the national press. Debate about the need to contextualize examination results in order to demonstrate the 'progress made by students from their level of performance on entry to their level of performance at the time they leave' emerged again with renewed vigour. With the Schools Bill, however, the DES, as indicated above, is demonstrating its opposition to any contextualization.

Overall trends in reporting

In terms of reporting to parents, the DES Circular and much of the text of its leaflet for teachers provide support for combining formative aspects of assessment into reporting procedures.

The design of the reporting format and the leaflet of advice to parents on school reports appear, however, to be emphasizing attainment levels. Such a position may further confuse teachers and downgrade the validity of teachers' assessments.

In terms of the National Record of Achievement, parental or student ownership emerges as an area where there is confusion. Wider issues about ownership are also present, but these are not within the scope of this chapter. It also appears to be the case that interest within the DES for a partnership with the Employment Department in developing the National Record of Achievement has waned. The handling of areas such as the appropriateness of the NRA for students with special educational needs is being left to the Employment Department, leaving many special schools anxious to know whether the DES is actively interested in their concerns.

Questions about individual student learning needs and the way schools meet those needs, of course, lie at the heart of the disquiet about the publication of school assessment results in order to make judgements about 'best' schools. At the time of writing, the impact of the use of raw results for judging school effectiveness cannot be fully gauged. Discussion, however, about the measures schools may feel obliged to take to improve the image of their overall results has already started.

Conclusion

The purpose of recording and reporting is to improve communication and understanding. The Secretary of State wrote to Professor Paul Black about TGAT's terms of reference in 1987:

> I attach considerable importance to improving communication and understanding at various levels about educational objectives and performance; information derived from assessment and testing will play a key part in that. (DES, 1988, Appendix B, p. 3)

The information derived from assessment and testing is ostensibly to be used both to support children's learning as well as to report individual progress and overall school performance. This chapter has portrayed some of the issues and trends which have emerged in implementing the use of such a unified assessment procedure. How much improvement in communication and understanding has resulted it is too soon to say.

References

Association for Science Education (1990) *Teacher Assessment: Making it Work for the Primary School*. ASE.

Brighouse, T. and Moon, B. (eds) (1990) *Managing the National Curriculum: Some Critical Perspectives*. Longman.

Christie, T. (1990) 'Monitoring the effectiveness of the National Curriculum: receiving and interpreting feedback.' In: Brighouse, T. and Moon, B. (eds) *Managing the National Curriculum: Some Critical Perspectives*. Longman.

DES (1988) *Task Group on Assessment and Testing: A Report*. DES/WO.

DES (1989) The Regulations (School Records) made under section 218 (1) (f) of the Education Reform Act. DES.

DES (1990) updated (1991) The Orders for Key Stage One (the Education (National Curriculum) Assessment Arrangements for English, Mathematics and Science Order). DES.

DES (1990) The Individual Pupils' Achievements (Information) Regulations. DES.

DES (1991) The Education (Information on School Examination Results) (England) Regulations. DES.

DES (1991) 'The Implementation of the Curricular Requirements of the Education Reform Act.' *Assessment, Recording and Reporting*. A Report by HMI on the First Year, 1989–90. DES.

DES (1991) The Parents' Charter.

Education (15 November 1991) p. 389 'The Parents' Bill of Rights'.

NCC (1991) Report on Monitoring the Implementation of the National Curriculum Core Subjects 1989–90.

Nuttall, D. (1989) 'National assessment – will reality match aspirations?' *BPS Education Section Review*, 13, 1-2.

Nuttall, D. (1991) 'An instrument to be honed.' *Times Educational Supplement*, 13 September 1991.

SEAC, (1990a) Criteria for LEA National Curriculum Assessment Implementation Plans. SEAC.

SEAC (1990b) A Guide to Teacher Assessment, Packs A, B and C. SEAC.

SEAC (1990/91) School Assessment Folder. SEAC.

SEAC (1991a) *Teacher Assessment at Key Stage 3*. SEAC.

SEAC (1991b) *National Curriculum Assessment: A Report on Teacher Assessment* by the NFER/BGC Consortium. SEAC.

University of Warwick (1991) *Workloads, Achievement and Stress*. Two follow-up studies of Teacher Time in Key Stage 1 1991. Commissioned by the Assistant Masters and Mistresses Association.

Chapter Eight
Whatever Happened to the TGAT Report?

Denis Lawton

I have a nice lecture on the Education Reform Act and the National Curriculum. I have given it many times in this country as well as in the USA, Australia, New Zealand, Hong Kong and Singapore. It is in three parts:

(1) Why we need a common, or 'entitlement', curriculum.
(2) Why I do not like the ERA National Curriculum.
(3) Why the assessment procedures as outlined in the TGAT Report made it possible to regard the National Curriculum as useful and worth while.

But I cannot use that paper any more: parts 1 and 2 are still true but, every month, changes are made to the assessment procedures which make it more and more difficult to be so optimistic about the survival of TGAT principles.

Nevertheless, I will try to find some positive aspects of the National Curriculum and its assessment. It is very easy, but unprofitable, simply to complain about the inadequacies and inconsistencies. I do realize that teachers have the task of trying to make the curriculum work however much they realize that the plan is imperfect and could have been much better.

National Curriculum
First of all, the National Curriculum is already much less an Entitlement Curriculum than even the 1988 Act seemed to promise: for Key Stage 4, the Secretary of State, Kenneth Clarke, ordained in January 1991 a new hierarchy of priorities for the 14 to 16 age group:

Core: English, mathematics and science (compulsory);
Extended Core: Technology, modern languages (still compulsory);
Choice: History and geography (entitlement reduced by 50 per cent);
Option: Art and music (entitlement reduced to the status of option);
Token: Physical education (will exist 'in some form').

Moreover, the curriculum structure has steadily become more subject-dominated since 1988. We now hear less and less about coherence and the integration of the whole curriculum, and very little about cross-curricular themes and skills. The current design reveals little concern for the whole curriculum 5–16 envisaged by HMI.

Assessment

The task of working out the details of an assessment scheme was in 1987 entrusted to Professor Paul Black and the Task Group for Assessment and Testing (TGAT). They did an amazing job in the six months allowed them and rushed a report to the Secretary of State on 24 December 1987. Their task would have been difficult enough had a purely educational model of assessment been required – but there were bureaucratic and political needs as well. There was a need to produce data for the DES which would show differences between schools and types of schools as well as trends over time; and some Conservative politicians wanted the kind of data which could enable parents to choose between good schools and bad schools – league tables. The result, the TGAT First Report (DES, 1988), was a remarkable document, but with several residual problems.

TGAT achievements

All major education reports have to some extent succeeded in changing public attitudes in some way: for example, Robbins on higher education and Plowden on primary education. The main achievements of TGAT were to produce significant changes in professional and public thinking in the following three areas:

(1)   moving the emphasis away from summative testing to formative assessment, incorporating a major role for teachers and sound recommendations about moderation;
(2)   moving discussion from 'absolute standards' to criterion referencing (of a non-doctrinaire kind); and
(3)   moving the debate away from fixed minimum standards (age-related benchmarks) to the flexibility of broadly defined Attainment Targets (ATs) with ten levels (with built-in progression and differentiation).

Each of these three achievements has been remarkable, but there were always difficulties which have been aggravated by changes in DES/Government policies, especially since October 1990, and changes in the School Examinations and Assessment Council (SEAC) since the summer of 1991. I will discuss the three headings in turn, although there are many links between them.

1. From summative tests to formative assessment
In 1987 (before TGAT) there was much hostility towards the idea of testing at age 7, and testing at 11 was seen as a revival of 11-plus selection. Further problems were raised about what to do with children who 'failed' the tests at 7, 11 or 14 – redoublement (repeating the year) or Boysonization (compulsory vacation classes)?

Instead, TAGT placed the emphasis on teacher assessment (TA), assessment integrated with good established teaching practices, and formative asssessment which might also become the first step in the process of diagnosing pupils' weaknesses.

But this left a number of problems. Standard Assessment Tasks (SATs) of the TGAT kind, it was realized, would be difficult to produce and would require plenty of time for trials and teacher preparation; the real timetable was political rather than educational. At the first sign of difficulty the Government has retreated to the ideologically more acceptable solution of short written tests. This intensifies the conflict between professional assessment and tests to be used for market choice.

2. From absolute standards to criterion-referencing (medium strength)
Joseph used the term 'absolute standards' in 1984. It was replaced in 1985 and 1987 by a word which rapidly became part of the professional teacher's vocabulary: criterion-referencing. TGAT retained it, but as a technical term it is not without its ambiguities and difficulties.

Criterion-referencing was in vogue with professional testers (not teachers) in the 1960s, but then fell out of fashion along with programmed learning and mastery teaching. Joseph needed a concept like it for what he wanted to say, but absolute standards would not do. Criterion-referencing is better but may not solve all the problems (Simpson, 1990). Part of Joseph's message was concerned with the difficult issues of standards which change over a period of time, as well as differences between subjects at any given time:

> We should move towards a greater degree of criterion-referencing...and away from norm-referencing. The existing system tells us a great deal about

relative standards between different candidates. It tells us much less about absolute standards. We lack clear definitions of the level of knowledge and performance expected from candidates for the award of particular grades. In mathematics 60 per cent of school leavers obtain a CSE Grade 4 or above. In English the figure is over 70 per cent. As the Cockcroft Committee pointed out, it is not clear whether the difference in these two levels reflects higher levels of attainment in English or higher expectations in mathematics... We need a reasonable assurance that pupils attaining a particular grade will know certain things and possess certain skills or have achieved a certain competence... We need... grade-related criteria...
(Sir Keith Joseph, 1984)

In principle, Joseph was surely right. In practice there are difficulties, and Desmond Nuttall (1988) at an early stage criticized the TGAT Report for regarding criterion-referencing as non-problematical.

It is not easy to find absolute standards anywhere in education. The most frequently quoted example of a test based on criteria is the driving test: a list of skills or competences on which a driver either passes or fails. But behind every criterion lurks a norm! How well does the candidate have to back round the corner? Do all examiners have precisely the same expectations? Does the same examiner always apply the criteria in exactly the same way? Before and after lunch?

In education, assessment is much more complex: there are fewer examples where it is possible to say 'yes or no' but it is often possible to make a judgement about more or less. Even where it is possible to turn a learning experience into a set of yes/no criteria, we may find teachers casting doubt on the validity of the exercise. For example, it is possible to have pupils learn the six-times table and pass a test where the criteria are very clear. But does parroting 'six times eight is 48' mean that the pupil can solve a real problem involving that process? In other words, is a test of rote-learning a valid way of assessing mathematical understanding? Politicians often assume that it is; if they looked at the evidence, they might be less certain.

Non-educationalists (including politicians) often appear to think it should be very easy to specify everything we want taught, break it down into little objectives (criteria), test them (right/wrong) and tick them off when they have been achieved. But there are two problems here: fragmentation (the Humpty Dumpty difficulty); and second, generalizability – the fact that it would be impossible to list every conceivable problem involving six times eight, so we have to make assumptions about transfer and draw the line where we think it is sensible.

In practice there are few examples of pure criteria. For that reason there is now more and more talk of 'strong' and 'weak' versions of criterion-referencing. Weaker (or less extreme) versions will tend to avoid 'pass/fail' because teachers realize that partial understanding is more likely than complete 'mastery'; this being the case, a teacher's judgement is all important. But with strong versions of criterion-referencing, judgement is unnecessary – competence, or mastery, speaks for itself.

Similarly, extreme (strong) versions of criterion-referencing will have no truck with the process of moderating teachers' standards – pass or fail should be completely clear and unambiguous. All public examinations including GCSE and A Levels employ moderation of some kind (and TGAT had useful comments to make about the types of moderation), but this has tended to fade away recently.

All of this is highly relevant to the future of National Curriculum assessment. The National Curriculum is a mixture of strong and weak criterion-referencing, and we need to know the difference. By 1994, GCSE grading also has to come into line with ten levels; all teachers must learn to be as specific as possible in their continuous assessment and Records of Achievement, but they may wish to avoid the temptation to apply strict criterion-referencing rules to everything.

3. From fixed age-related benchmarks to ATs with ten levels
In 1987 we were apprehensive about benchmarks, pass/fail testing and redoublement. Instead, TGAT produced ten levels with an emphasis on individual progression, avoiding the crude and unsatisfactory categories of 'below average' or 'fail'. Within the TGAT assessment model, progression is individual and developmental (ipsative) rather than competitive (rank-ordered).

Paul Black was able to make use of the experience and the evidence of 'graded assessment' work, much of it carried out from King's College London. To have ten levels is in one sense arbitrary, but it is a real advantage to avoid a one-level, one-year norm which would have encouraged the tendency to exaggerate the link between age and achievement which spoils many systems. The essence of graded assessment is that students are encouraged to progress individually, at their own pace, rather than in lock-step with the rest of the class or age group. Many advantages have been pointed out: clear progression, good task-orientation for the pupils, improving motivation, and differentiation – a variety of abilities (or learning speeds) – is catered for.

The TGAT Report represented a compromise. It contains some of the advantages of graded assessment whilst providing the bureaucratic data required by the Department of Education and Science (DES) and, more regrettably, the data required by politicians for market choice.

The future of the TGAT model

It should have been realized in 1988 that satisfactory implementation of the TGAT Report would have required a long-term research and development programme. But this was not on the political agenda and TGAT is now in danger of being completely distorted for short-term political reasons.

There are at least six problems of National Curriculum assessment which will need to be carefully addressed during the 1990s:

(1) levels;
(2) progression;
(3) the subject – profile component (PC)/AT/Statement of Attainment (SoA) relationship;
(4) aggregation;
(5) competition; and
(6) league tables.

Levels

The concept of 'level' is a major feature of the TGAT Report. But assessment experts are divided on the question of validity and appropriateness of levels as a model for learning. The research in favour of levels has come from graded assessment. It is too early to have much evidence from the National Curriculum pilot studies. Margaret Brown and her colleagues claim that despite difficulties it is useful to plan a curriculum in this way (Brown, 1989).

On the other hand, Goldstein and others are very critical of the concept (Noss, *et al.*, 1989). The dispute revolves around another concept – 'hierarchy' – the assumption that achievement of everything that is required, say, for level 3, implies capability of achieving everything required for the lower levels. There are two interrelated questions here: (1) is the subject structured in that way? and (2) do children learn like that? (which is related to questions of progression).

There is another important question: are *all subjects* capable of being split into the same ten levels? If so, are the levels so far produced truly comparable from one subject to another? (There are some inconsistencies, for example, between maths and science.) A good deal of work needs to be done to map out the precise nature of levels and progression in each subject.

Progression
Issues about level are closely related to the notion of progression which was also emphasized in the TGAT Report. Critics suggest that learning does not take place in a strictly cumulative way, and learning sequences differ from one individual to another. Margaret Brown acknowledges the reasons for the doubt and reminds teachers that AT levels should not be used to plan teaching/learning sequences; nevertheless, the levels are useful as a rough, overall guide to progress. Models are always neater than reality, and good teachers may find the levels useful as a guide, but will be flexible in using them.

The subject/PC/AT/SoA relationship
Quite apart from the question of levels, there is another set of questions about the relation between subjects, profile components, Attainment Targets and Statements of Attainment. It is quite clear that the different subject Working Groups interpreted their brief differently (even given possible differences in the structure of the subjects), especially the PC/AT relationship. The result, in 1991, was the virtual elimination of PC from the model, and the consequent elevation of ATs. In the context of that discussion it was suggested that there were too many ATs in both mathematics and science, and new Working Groups were set up to reduce them. But this raises new questions about the tension between the desire to be as specific as possible and the danger of being over-specific. This has been a contentious issue in curriculum studies for at least 30 years. It is just not possible to reduce the number of ATs in mathematics (e.g. from 14 to 5) without making the ATs and the SoAs more general.

Aggregation
There are at least two problems here: (1) the complexity of the task of aggregating scores from SoA to AT to subject; and (2) the validity of the result (i.e. if you add them up, using whatever formula is required, does it provide an answer which could be regarded as reasonable?).

Both problems exist at KS1 and KS3, and will also arise at KS2 and KS4. The transition from GCSE grades to National Curriculum levels in 1994 will present technical difficulties which politicians and DES officials have chosen to ignore.

Competition
Among pupils: the spirit of TGAT is ipsative; the reality may however be unhealthy competition. Parents, for example, might be tempted to buy all the books listed as approved for assessing KS1 Reading.

Among teachers: competition may obstruct completely professional behaviour and attitudes. Teachers might be tempted to grade generously, and underplay their diagnostic role.

Among schools: some headteachers may be tempted to play the market game in the search for more pupils instead of putting the published results into a context, and explaining the multi-causality of 'good' results.

League tables
Secondary schools have been obliged to publish examination results since 1982 (1980 Education Act). In 1990 Desmond Nuttall could show that parents did not choose schools using that criterion as the most important factor (discipline and proximity were given higher priority). But in January 1991, Michael Fallon, Parliamentary Under-Secretary of State for Education and Science, published not only a league table of LEAs according to what percentage of school leavers had five or more subjects with A, B or C, but also related these results to high and low spending LEAs in a completely misleading and blatantly political way (which caused Stuart Maclure (1991) to write a very angry article in the *TES*). The Parents Charter (1991) now attempts to make league tables respectable. They are not. But there is likely to be political pressure on schools and LEAs to play the league table game at KS1, 2 and 3, despite the fact that professionally we know what nonsense this is. The agenda for the 1990s ought to include a better way of evaluating schools than looking at crude test scores (Goldstein, 1987).

Conclusion
Much of the TGAT Report has already been lost, but there is still a good deal to fight for. The future could be either a gradual return to the positive aspects of professional assessment, or a further retreat to bureaucratic testing. At the moment there are signs of continued pressure from right wing 'think tanks'. A recent propaganda document from the Social Market Foundation – *Standards in Schools* (1991) by John Marks, of the Centre for Policy Studies – is highly critical of TGAT and urges a return to conventional tests. The fact that he has recently been made a member of SEAC will increase his influence. On a previous occasion, a right wing assault on TGAT was made via the Prime Minister's Office in 1988

(Lawton, 1989, pp. 58–9). Kenneth Baker on that occasion stood up to the Prime Minister's far-right advisers and TGAT survived. Now the attack is focusing attention on costs and, although John Marks' figures are open to question, the idea of shorter and cheaper tests and the complete abolition of TGAT might appeal to the newly elected Conservative Government.

References

Brown, M. (1989) 'Graded Assessment and Learning Hierarchies in Mathematics: An Alternative View.' *British Education Research Journal*, Vol. 15.2, pp. 121–8.

Department of Education and Science and the Welsh Office (1988a) *National Curriculum: Task Group on Assessment and Testing: A Report*. DES/WO.

Department of Education and Science and the Welsh Office (1988b) *National Curriculum: Three Supplementary Reports – Task Group on Assessment and Testing*. DES/WO.

Department of Education and Science and the Welsh Office (1988c) *National Curriculum: Task Group on Assessment and Testing Report – A Digest for Schools*. DES/WO.

Joseph, Sir Keith (1984) Secretary of State's speech to the North of England Conference, DES press release.

Goldstein, H. (1987) *Multilevel Models in Educational and Social Research*. London: Charles Griffin

Lawton, D. (1989) *Education, Culture and the National Curriculum*. London: Hodder & Stoughton.

Marks, J. (Centre for Policy Studies) (1991) *Standards in Schools*. London: Social Market Foundation.

Maclure, S. (1991) 'A PUSS: into bootless talk.' In: *The Times Educational Supplement*, Friday, 25 January 1991. London: The Times Supplements Ltd.

Noss, R., *et al.* (1989) 'Graded Assessment and Learning Hierarchies in Mathematics.' *British Education Research Journal*, Vol. 15.2, pp. 109–120.

Nuttall, D. (1988) 'National Assessment.' In: Lawton, D. (1988) *The Education Reform Act: Choice and Control*. London: Hodder & Stoughton.

Nuttall, D. (1990) *Differences in Examination Performance*. London: Inner London Education Authority R. & S. Branch.

Simpson, M. (1990) 'Why Criterion-Referencing is Unlikely to Improve Learning.' *The Curriculum Journal*, Vol. 1, No. 2.